VISUAL QUICKSTART GUIDE

iPad

CHRIS FEHILY

Visual QuickStart Guide
iPad
Chris Fehily

Peachpit Press
1249 Eighth Street
Berkeley, CA 94710
510/524-2178
510/524-2221 (fax)

Find us on the Web at www.peachpit.com.
To report errors, please send a note to errata@peachpit.com.
Peachpit Press is a division of Pearson Education.

Executive editor: Clifford Colby
Editor: Kathy Simpson
Production editor: Cory Borman
Compositor: David Van Ness
Indexer: Valerie Haines Perry
Cover design: RHDG / Riezebos Holzbaur Design Group, Peachpit Press
Interior design: Peachpit Press
Logo design: MINE™ www.minesf.com

Notice of Rights

Notice of Liability

Trademarks

ISBN-13: 978-0-321-84259-6
ISBN-10: 0-321-84259-6

9 8 7 6 5 4 3 2 1

Printed and bound in the United States of America

Contents at a Glance

Table of Contents

1

Getting Started

You've seen the TV ads in which happy, purposeful people use iPads to type messages, watch movies, play games, video-chat with grandchildren, and surf the Web from hammocks. On the cutting-room floor, however, is the footage where those actors actually *learned* how to do all that stuff. Despite its clean lines and compact size, the iPad is a true computer running complex programs on a modern operating system. Happily, Apple's engineers have painted a pretty face on all the gee-whizzery. The iPad's consistent, simple design lets you wield a lot of power with only a little learning. Even complete beginners can't easily shoot themselves in the foot. This chapter gets you up and running.

In This Chapter

Hardware and Specifications

The iPad's physical controls and ports (A and B) are covered in detail later in this chapter and beyond. You can refer to these figures to jog your memory. Some 4G/3G models (for connecting to cellular networks) have a micro-SIM card slot on the left edge. The iPad 1 has no front and back cameras.

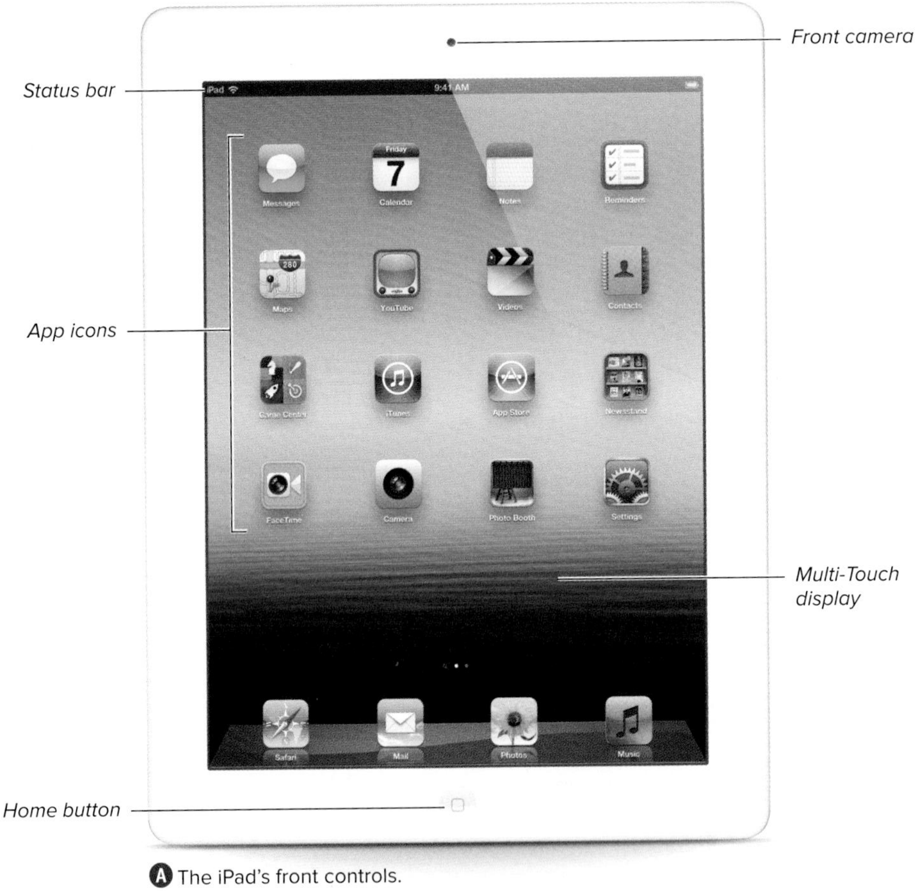

A The iPad's front controls.

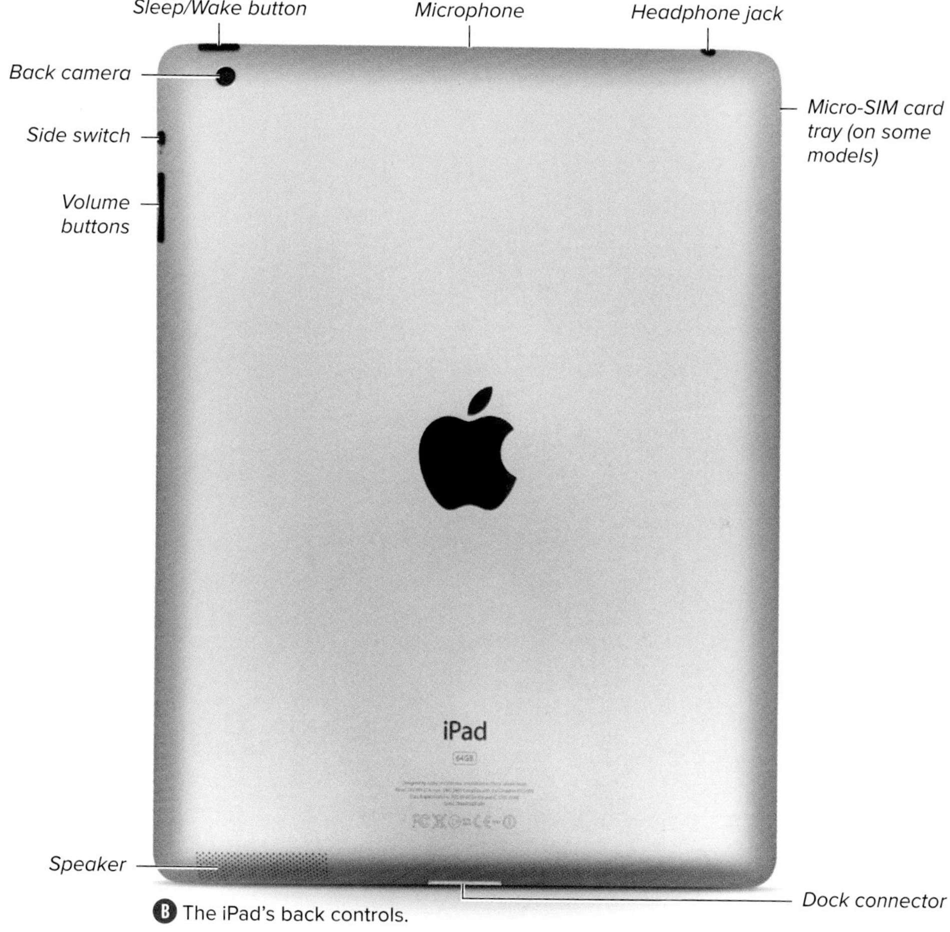

B The iPad's back controls.

At this writing, Apple sells the iPad 2 (discounted from its original list price) and the iPad 3 (which Apple calls the "new iPad" or "third-generation iPad"). **Table 1.1** lists some key specifications for these models. For a complete list, see http://support.apple.com/kb/SP647.

The iPad also comes with:

- A *10W USB power adapter,* used to provide power and charge the battery. (Don't use a different power adapter to charge your iPad.)
- A *dock connector–to–USB cable,* used to connect your iPad to the 10W USB power adapter or to your computer to sync with iTunes.

TIP The iPad's operating system, called *iOS,* is the same OS that also runs the iPhone, iPod touch, and Apple TV.

TABLE 1.1 iPad Specifications

Specification	iPad 3	iPad 2
Dimensions	9.50" × 7.31" × 0.37" (241.2mm × 185.7mm × 9.4mm)	9.50" × 7.31" × 0.34" (241.2mm × 185.7mm × 8.8mm)
Weight	1.44 pounds (652 g)	1.33 pounds (601 g)
Display size	9.7" (246mm) diagonal	9.7" (246mm) diagonal
Display resolution	2048 × 1536 pixels (264 pixels per inch)	1024 × 768 pixels (132 pixels per inch)
Processors	1 GHz dual-core A5X with quad-core graphics	1 GHz dual-core A5 with dual-core graphics
Memory (RAM)	1 GB	512 MB
Storage	16, 32, or 64 GB	16 GB
Wireless	Wi-Fi only or Wi-Fi+4G	Wi-Fi only or Wi-Fi+3G
Battery life	Up to 10 hours Wi-Fi Up to 9 hours 4G	Up to 10 hours Wi-Fi Up to 9 hours 3G
Back camera	5 megapixels	0.92 megapixels

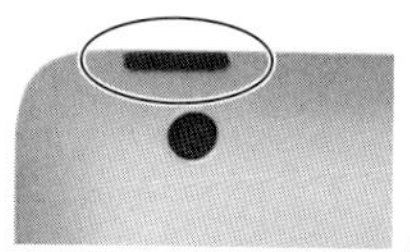

A Use the Sleep/Wake button at the iPad's top edge to blank the screen and save power.

B The iPad locks itself because, as with any touchscreen device, an unintended tap on the screen while it's in your bag or backpack can launch a program and drain the battery.

Shorthand Instructions

Throughout this book, you'll find shorthand instructions like "Tap Settings > General > Wi-Fi > On," which means this: On the Home screen, tap the Settings app, tap General (on the left), and then slide Wi-Fi to On. Each name between the > symbols refers to an app, icon, button, link, or control; just look on the screen for a matching label.

Smart Covers

If you have an iPad Smart Cover, sold separately by Apple, you can use it to automatically sleep or wake an iPad 2 or later when you open or close the flap. The cover interacts with magnets built into the iPad's case to align the cover and provide the sleep/wake feature. To change this behavior, tap Settings > General > iPad Cover Lock/Unlock.

Powering On and Off

Putting an iPad to sleep locks it in standby mode: The screen turns off and doesn't respond to taps, but audio keeps playing, and the volume buttons still work. The battery drains slowly but noticeably. A sleeping iPad wakes instantly to where you left off. You may also need to wake your iPad if you leave it untended for a few minutes, because it goes to sleep by itself to save power.

Powering off an iPad shuts it down: No power is used, though the battery still drains imperceptibly over days or weeks. A powered-off iPad takes a minute to power on and show the Home screen.

TIP In day-to-day use, you don't need to power off; sleep suffices in most cases.

To put your iPad to sleep:

- Press the Sleep/Wake button **A**.

To wake your iPad:

- Press the Home button or the Sleep/Wake button and then drag the slider **B**.

TIP To adjust how long your iPad screen stays on before it turns itself off (and displays the Lock screen when you wake it up), tap Settings > General > Auto-Lock.

To power off your iPad:

- Press and hold the Sleep/Wake button for a few seconds until a red slider appears and then drag the slider.

To power on your iPad:

- Press and hold the Sleep/Wake button until the Apple logo appears.

TIP To set a security passcode that you must enter each time you wake or power on your iPad, see "Securing Your iPad" later in this chapter.

Quick Fixes

The iPad does a good job of fixing its own problems, but it can accumulate software baggage with time and use. *Restarting* your iPad (powering it off and then back on) can quickly solve many common problems, including unexpected app failure, short battery life, odd hardware behavior, slow app or iOS response, and iTunes sync issues. A restart does all the following:

- Safely quits all active applications and processes and closes all open files, preserving your data
- Frees CPU and memory (RAM) resources
- Powers off all hardware components

A restart may fail on a crashed or frozen iPad. If you can't restart your iPad, *reset* it: Press and hold the Sleep/Wake button and the Home button at the same time for at least 10 seconds, until the Apple logo appears, and then release both buttons. A reset halts all power briefly and doesn't close open files or save data before rebooting your iPad (that is, you lose any unsaved data).

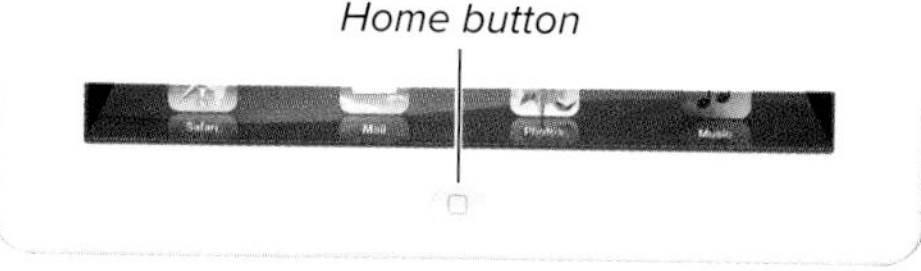

Ⓐ You'll probably use the Home button more than any other iPad switch.

Using the Home Button

The only physical control on the front of the iPad is the *Home button* Ⓐ. It's the round, indented switch at the bottom center of the iPad frame (called the *bezel*). The Home button handles a few tasks. Most important, it always zips you straight to the Home screen—the iPad's main screen, where you find all your apps (programs).

Because the iPad displays only one app at a time, you can use the Home button to switch among apps. If you're browsing the Web in Safari, for example, when your iPad chimes an incoming-email alert, press the Home button to close Safari and go back to the Home screen, where you can tap the Mail icon to read your email.

Pressing Home always saves your work in progress automatically. (Unlike Windows and OS X programs, iPad apps have no manual Save command.) If you're typing a list in the Notes app and then press Home, you can return to Notes at any time, exactly as you left off.

TIP Double-clicking the Home button lets you switch among your active apps quickly. For details, see "Opening and Switching Apps" later in this chapter.

Using Multitouch Gestures

The iPad is designed for your fingertips. You interact with the software on the screen by performing the *multitouch gestures* described in **Table 1.2**. If you've used a computer mouse, learning these gestures will be easy because tapping and dragging correspond to similar mouse actions. Unfamiliar motions like flicking and pinching quickly become natural.

TIP If you have vision, hearing, or mobility problems, tap Settings > General > Accessibility to make your iPad easier to use.

TABLE 1.2 Multitouch Gestures

To	Do This
Tap	Gently tap the screen with one finger.
Double-tap	Tap twice quickly. (If you tap too slowly, your iPad interprets your action as two single taps.) A double tap is a quick way to zoom in on a photo or Web page or to toggle a video between full-screen and widescreen (letterbox) aspect ratios.
Touch and hold	Touch the screen with your finger, and maintain contact with the glass (typically, until some onscreen action happens).
Drag	Touch and hold a point on the screen; then slide your finger across the glass to a different part of the screen. A draglike slide moves a control along a constrained path. You slide the iPad's unlock and volume sliders, for example.
Flick (or swipe)	Fluidly and decisively whip your finger across the screen. If you're on a Web page or a list, a faster flick scrolls the screen faster.
Pinch	Touch your thumb and index finger to the screen; then pinch them together (to zoom out) or spread them apart (to zoom in).
Rotate	Spread your thumb and index finger and touch them to the screen; then rotate them clockwise or counterclockwise. (Or keep your fingers steady and rotate the iPad itself.)

Shake It

You can shake your iPad. The iPad's accelerometer recognizes an intentional shaking motion. Shaking front to back works better than shaking side to side. Some apps recognize a shake and respond to it. Shaking while you're typing in Notes, for example, opens a box that lets you undo your last action.

The iPad's *capacitive* screen contains a dense grid of touch sensors that responds to the electric field of your fingers. The screen won't respond to a stylus (and you can't wear gloves). Increasing finger pressure on a capacitive screen, as opposed to a resistive screen, won't increase responsiveness.

Feel free to use two hands. You can use both hands to type on the iPad's onscreen keyboard, for example. In some apps (such as Apple's iWork apps), you can touch and hold an item with one hand and then use your other hand to tap other items to select them all as a group. If you're having trouble with a gesture, make sure that you're not touching the screen's edge with a stray thumb or finger (of either hand).

TIP Some apps, such as Contacts, use index lists (A, B, C,...) along an edge to help you navigate quickly. To scroll though an a index, drag your finger along it, or tap a letter to jump to items starting with that letter. Tap an item to open it. In some apps, a back button in the top-left corner takes you back to the index.

Setting Up Your iPad

The first thing to do with a new, out-of-the-box iPad is set it up. To do so, you need a nearby wireless Internet connection. (Don't wander away from the Wi-Fi signal with your iPad during setup.) Your iPad will also need a significant battery charge if the battery drained while sitting in the cargo container or on the store shelf; see "Charging the Battery" later in this chapter.

TIP You don't need a computer and iTunes to set up your iPad, as you did with iOS 4 or earlier. If you *do* use iTunes, you'll need to connect your iPad to a Mac or Windows PC running iTunes via the USB cable that came with your iPad. The Setup Assistant will offer you iTunes-specific sync and backup options. See also "Syncing with iTunes" in Chapter 4.

Selling Your Old iPad

Before you sell or give away an iPad, erase all its content and settings so that the new owner can't access your stuff. Erasing an iPad lets you return it to its factory settings without reinstalling iOS.

To erase your iPad, tap Settings > General > Reset > Erase All Content and Settings. The process takes a few minutes. The iPad supports hardware encryption, so it needs only to remove the encryption key that protects your data. (It doesn't need to overwrite all your data with garbage data, which would take hours.)

If you want something less severe than a complete data wipe, you can change the iPad settings back to their default factory values but not erase your content. To do so, tap Settings > General > Reset > Reset All Settings. The affected settings include the Home-screen layout, built-in apps, Settings app, passcode, network settings, keyboard dictionary, and other odds and ends. Settings for third-party apps aren't changed, and no data or media are deleted.

Charge the battery before a reset. To use iCloud or iTunes to back up your data before a reset, see Chapter 4.

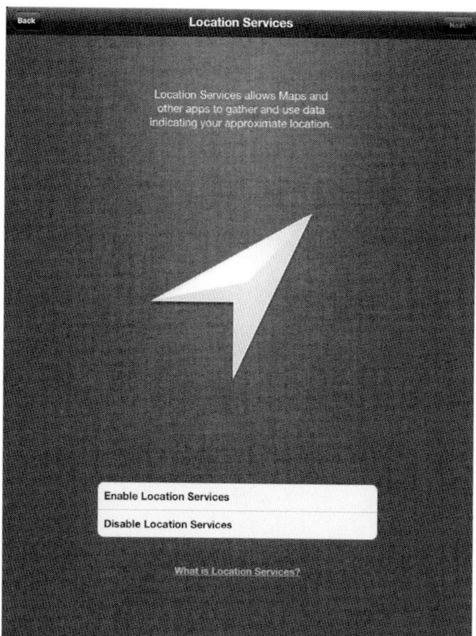

A Location Services lets built-in apps such as Maps and Safari and third-party apps such as weather apps use your physical whereabouts via the iPad's built-in positioning service.

B Your Apple ID is a unique online user name and password that lets you use iCloud, FaceTime, Game Center, Apple online stores, Find My iPad, and other Apple apps and services.

To set up your new iPad, turn it on and then follow the onscreen instructions. The Setup Assistant steps you through the setup process. Along the way, you're asked to:

- Choose your preferred language for the iPad's screens, keyboard, and interface.
- Pick your country or region.
- Turn on Location Services **A**. For details, see "Location Services" in Chapter 3.
- Connect to a Wi-Fi network. A secured home network is safer than a public network at a café or library, where miscreant geeks can sniff out your passwords and personal information as you type. For details, see "Making Wi-Fi Connections" in Chapter 3.
- Choose whether to set up your device as a new iPad or restore it from an iCloud or iTunes backup. (For backups, see the iCloud and iTunes sections in Chapter 4.)
- Sign in with or create an Apple ID **B**.

continues on next page

- Set up iCloud **C**. For details, see "Using iCloud" in Chapter 4.
- Use dictation, which converts what you say to text when you tap the microphone button on the keyboard (in any app that uses a keyboard). For details, see "Using the Onscreen Keyboard" in Chapter 2.
- Send daily diagnostics and use data to Apple. (Don't bother; save the bandwidth.)
- Register your iPad with Apple, if you want to. (It's unnecessary.)
- Agree to terms and conditions for using iPad, iCloud, and other services.

When you're done, tap Start Using iPad to go to the Home screen, where you can see all the iPad's built-in apps: Safari, Mail, Calendar, Notes, Maps, and more.

TIP If you change your mind or skip a step during setup, you can change the setup options later by using the Settings app. To toggle Location Services, for example, tap Settings > Location Services. To sign in to, change, or create an Apple ID, tap Settings > Store. To change iCloud settings, tap Settings > iCloud. To set up Internet-based mail and other accounts, tap Settings > Mail, Contacts, Calendars.

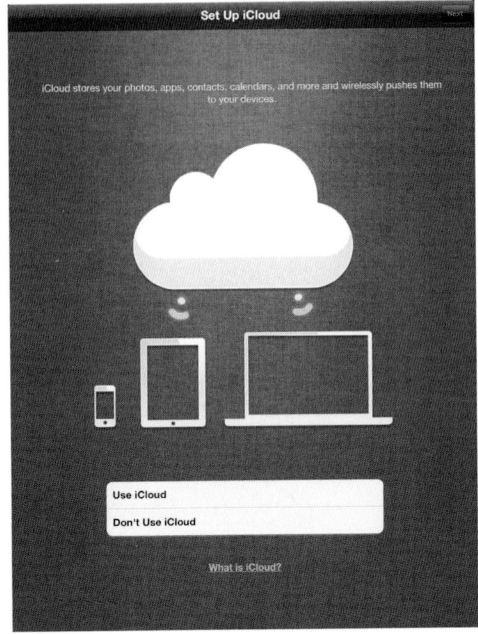

C Apple's free iCloud service lets you automatically sync contacts, calendars, email, photos, and documents across your Mac, Windows PC, iPad, and other iDevices (if you own more than one). You can also use iCloud to back up your apps, settings, and content to Apple's online servers, and restore your iPad from this backup.

Navigating the Home Screen

After you unlock your iPad, the *Home screen* appears, displaying icons for your applications, or *apps* **A**. The iPad comes with several built-in apps (Safari, Mail, and Settings, for example), and you can download more from the App Store, Apple's online store for iOS applications. If you install lots of apps, new Home screens sprout automatically to display them.

Put your most frequently used apps in the *dock*, which is visible at the bottom of every Home screen and holds up to six icons. The row of small dots above the dock indicates how many screens you have and which one you're on. (You can create up to 11 Home screens.) You can customize the layout of app icons on the Home screen and in the dock.

A The Home screen.

To show the Home screen:

- Press the Home button.

  or

  Use four or five fingers to pinch to the Home screen.

TIP To toggle the multitouch gesture for the Home screen, tap Settings > General > Multitasking Gestures.

To switch Home screens:

- Flick left or right.

  or

  Tap to the left or right of the dots above the dock.

  or

  To go to the first Home screen, press the Home button.

To rearrange Home-screen icons:

1. Touch and hold any app icon for a few seconds until all the icons wiggle.
2. Drag icons to new locations within a screen or off the edge of one screen and onto the next.
3. Press the Home button to stop the wiggling and save your arrangement.

TIP You can also rearrange Home-screen icons (as well as the order of the screens) in iTunes on your computer. To do so, connect your iPad to your computer via USB cable, open iTunes on your computer, select your iPad in the iTunes sidebar, and then click the Apps tab.

Viewing the Status Bar

The *status bar* is the narrow strip that runs along the top of the Home screen, the Lock screen, and many application screens **A**.

A A glance at the status bar can tell you whether all is well with your iPad.

Date & Time

The time of day appears in the center of the status bar (unless it's replaced by the screen-lock icon). By default, the time and time zone are set automatically, based on your Internet connection. By tapping Settings > General > Date & Time **B**, you can switch between the 12-hour (AM/PM) or 24-hour clock. If you're traveling, you can choose a time zone and set your iPad's date and time manually.

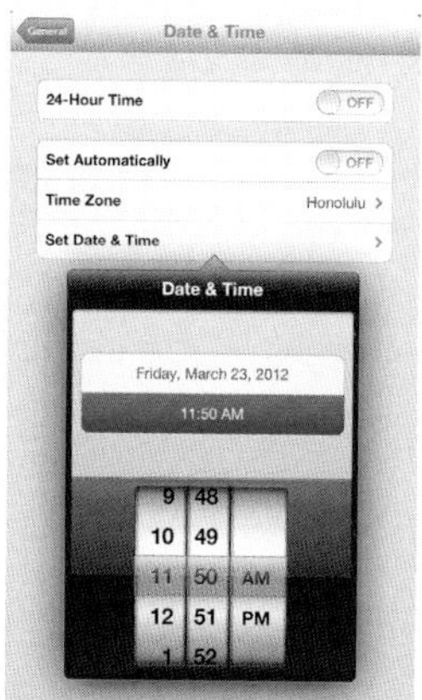

B The Date & Time screen.

The status bar shows the current time and displays icons that indicate the current state of your iPad, including the following:

- Airplane mode is on
- **4G** Cellular network availability, including icons for 3G, 4G, LTE, E (for EDGE), and **O** (for GPRS)
- Wi-Fi network connectivity and signal strength
- Personal hotspot provided
- iTunes sync in progress
- Network or other activity
- **VPN** VPN network connectivity
- iPad is screen-locked (replaces clock)
- Screen orientation is locked
- Location Services is in use
- Music, audiobook, or other media is playing
- Bluetooth is turned on and paired with a device
- Battery level or charging status

TIP Keep your iPad's time accurate; apps use it to time-stamp files and messages, schedule tasks, and record events.

Creating Home-Screen Folders

If too many icons are crowding your Home screens, you can group them into folders rather than drag them around to different screens. Each folder can hold up to 20 icons. It's a common practice to create multiple folders, each holding similar types of apps (games, music, travel, and so on). Folders save a lot of screen space and reduce excessive screen-switching.

To create a folder:

1. Touch and hold an icon until it wiggles; then drag it on top of an icon that you want to store in the same folder.

   The iPad creates a new folder containing the two icons **A**.

2. Accept the default folder name, or tap the name field to type a new name.

   The onscreen keyboard appears when you tap the name.

3. Tap outside the folder to close it **B**.

To open a folder:

- Tap the folder; then tap an app icon in the folder to open that app.

TIP If you have lots of folders and forget where you put an app, flick left to right as far as you can go (to the Spotlight search screen) and then search for the app.

A The iPad automatically names a new folder based on the icons that you use to create it.

B A folder appears on the Home screen as a black box containing tiny icons.

To close a folder:

- Tap outside the folder, or press the Home button.

To add an icon to a folder:

1. Touch and hold the icon until it wiggles; then drag it on top of the folder.
2. If you like, drag other icons to the folder (or to other folders), or drag icons within a folder to rearrange them.
3. When you're done, press the Home button to stop the wiggling and save your arrangement.

To remove an icon from a folder:

1. Tap the folder to open it.
2. Touch and hold the icon until it wiggles.
3. Drag the icon out of the folder.

To delete a folder:

1. Tap the folder to open it.
2. Touch and hold any icon until it wiggles.
3. Drag all the icons out of the folder.

   The folder disappears when you remove the last icon.

To rename a folder:

1. Tap the folder to open it.
2. Touch and hold any icon until it wiggles.
3. Tap the name field.
4. Type a new name when the onscreen keyboard appears.

TIP You can reset the Home screen to its original layout to remove any folders that you've created (and apply the Home screen's default wallpaper). To do so, tap Settings > General > Reset > Reset Home Screen Layout.

Opening and Switching Apps

The iPad displays only one app at a time, full-screen. You can't have, say, Safari on one side of the screen and Mail on the other, as you can in Windows or OS X. Fortunately, the iPad supports *multitasking*—which lets multiple apps run in the background at the same time—and you can quickly open, switch among, and close apps.

Most apps are effectively frozen when you switch away from them, but certain apps (such as Music and Mail) continue working in the background. Switching back to an app lets you resume where you left off.

To open an app:

- Tap its icon.

To switch to an app:

- Press the Home button and then tap the app's icon on the Home screen. (You can also pinch with four or five fingers to go to the Home screen.)

  or

  Double-click the Home button to show the *multitasking bar* at the bottom of the screen; then tap the app's icon **A**. You may have to flick left to find it. (You can also show or hide the multitasking bar by flicking up or down with four or five fingers.)

  or

  Flick left or right with four or five fingers to switch to the next or previous app.

TIP To toggle multitouch gestures for multitasking, tap Settings > General > Multitasking Gestures.

A The Home screen scrolls up to reveal the multitasking bar, which lists your recently used apps.

Alert Badges

Some apps try to get your attention by displaying an *alert badge*—a number in a little red circle superimposed on the app's Home-screen icon **B**. The number is the count of new, unread, or unattended items for that app. Mail shows the number of incoming mail messages, for example; App Store shows the number of apps that need to be updated; and Newsstand shows the number of new issues.

B If the app is in a folder, the badge appears on the folder as well.

Some apps use alert badges in novel ways. At least one weather app uses an alert badge to show the outdoor temperature.

A badge with an exclamation point (!) indicates a problem with the app.

Closing Apps

If the multitasking bar gets too crowded, making you scroll long distances to find an app, you can close apps that you haven't used recently and purge their icons from the list.

Also, if an app is unresponsive or freezes when it opens, and pressing the Home button doesn't work, you can force-quit the app to return to the Home screen.

To close an app:

1. Show the multitasking bar, as described in "To switch to an app" earlier in this chapter.
2. Touch and hold an icon until it wiggles and then tap ⊖.

   The app closes, and its icon is removed from the recently used list (but not from the iPad itself).
3. If you like, close other apps.
4. When you're done, press the Home button to stop the wiggling.

TIP In most cases, closing apps does little to conserve power or memory.

To force-quit a frozen app:

1. Press and hold the Sleep/Wake button until the power-off screen appears and then release the Sleep/Wake button.

   Don't drag the red slider.
2. Press and hold the Home button for 6 seconds, until the Home screen appears.
3. If the Home screen doesn't appear, restart your iPad by repeating step 1, but this time, drag the red slider.

Adjusting Screen Brightness

You can make the iPad's screen brighter or dimmer, or have the iPad adjust screen brightness automatically for ambient light.

To adjust screen brightness:

1. Tap Settings > Brightness & Wallpaper **A**.
2. To adjust brightness manually, drag the slider.

   or

   To make the iPad autoadjust brightness for current light conditions, turn on Auto-Brightness.

TIP A quick way to adjust screen brightness: Double-click the Home button to show the multitasking bar at the bottom of the screen, flick left to right, and then drag the brightness slider.

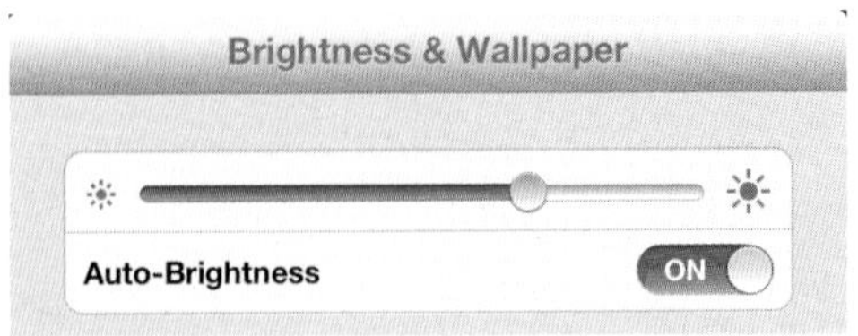

A If you're going to read for a long time, a dim screen is less fatiguing than a bright one.

The Ambient Light Sensor

When Auto-Brightness is turned on, the iPad autoadjusts brightness by using its built-in ambient light sensor. This sensor, located near the front camera, is barely visible behind the screen's bezel. If the screen doesn't dim automatically, check whether something (your hand, a protective film, or a case) is blocking or obscuring the sensor.

Some apps, such as iBooks, have their own screen-brightness slider that overrides the Settings slider.

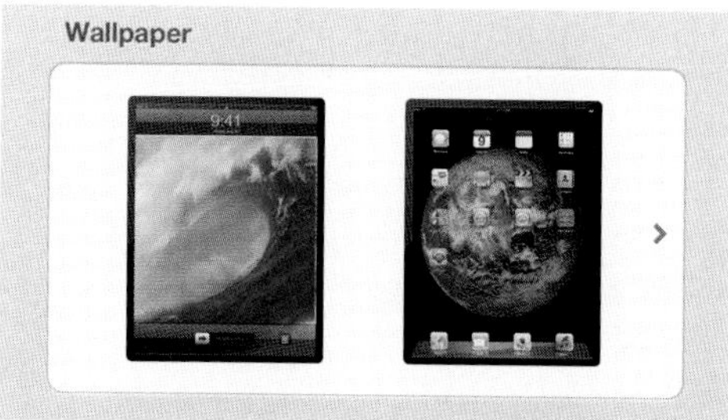

Ⓐ You can choose separate images for the Home screen and the Lock screen.

Changing the Wallpaper

You can choose the photo or image that you want to use as a background image, or *wallpaper*, for your Home screen or Lock screen. (The Lock screen is the one you see when you first wake or turn on your iPad.)

The iPad comes with some high-resolution stock images (mostly nature scenes and textured patterns) for use as wallpaper, but you can use a photo from your own photo albums.

To change the wallpaper:

1. Tap Settings > Brightness & Wallpaper.
2. Tap the small Wallpaper images Ⓐ.
3. Tap Wallpaper (to use one of Apple's stock images) or tap Saved Photos (to use your own photo).
4. Tap the image that you want to use.
5. (Optional) If you chose one of your own photos, you can pinch two fingers together (to zoom out) or spread them apart (to zoom in) and drag the image around to choose the part that you want to display.
6. Tap Set Lock Screen, Set Home Screen, or Set Both.

   or

   To keep your current wallpaper, tap Cancel.

Changing Screen Orientation

The iPad's built-in accelerometer senses how you're holding the iPad in physical space and then orients the screen to either portrait (tall) or landscape (wide) view **A**.

To change the view, rotate the iPad. The Home screen, the Lock screen, and most apps self-adjust to fit the new orientation. (Some apps support only one view. Many games, for example, work only in landscape view.)

If you don't want the screen to change its orientation, such as when you're reading while lying down, you can lock the current view to stop it from rotating. You have two ways to do so:

- **Use the side switch.** The side switch is the toggle switch next to the volume buttons **B**. You can set it to lock/unlock screen rotation or mute/unmute the sound. To make the iPad lock rotation, tap Settings > General and then tap Lock Rotation (below the words *Use Side Switch To*). When you choose this option, the opposite option (Mute) becomes available in the multitasking bar.
- **Use the multitasking bar.** Double-click the Home button to show the multitasking bar at the bottom of the screen **C**, flick left to right, and then tap 🔒.

TIP This option is available only if you've set the side switch to Mute; to do so, tap Settings > General.

When you lock rotation, a rotation overlay appears briefly onscreen, and the 🔒 icon appears in the status bar at the top of the screen.

A The same Web page in portrait and landscape views. In Safari, Web pages scale automatically to the wider screen, making the text and images larger.

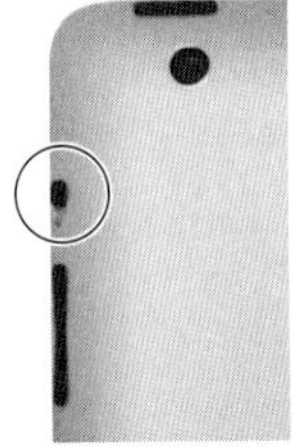

B The side switch.

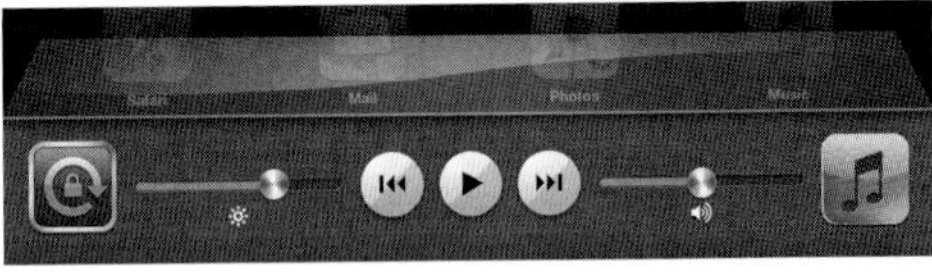

C The leftmost button in the multitasking bar either locks orientation or mutes audio, depending on the side-switch setting.

Adjusting the Volume

The buttons on the right edge of the iPad control the volume **A**.

- **Volume buttons.** The volume control is a rocker switch with two buttons that adjust the audio level of anything that makes noise, such as songs, videos, audiobooks, podcasts, apps, alerts, and sound effects. Volume adjustments affect the iPad's built-in speaker, earphones or headsets plugged into the headphone jack, and external speakers connected wirelessly or through the dock connector. An audio-level overlay appears briefly onscreen as you adjust the volume.
- **Side switch.** The side switch is a toggle switch that, by default, mutes the sound when you slide it down. If you don't need a Mute button, you can set the side switch to lock screen rotation instead: Tap Settings > General and then tap Lock Rotation **B**. For details, see "Changing Screen Orientation" earlier in this chapter.

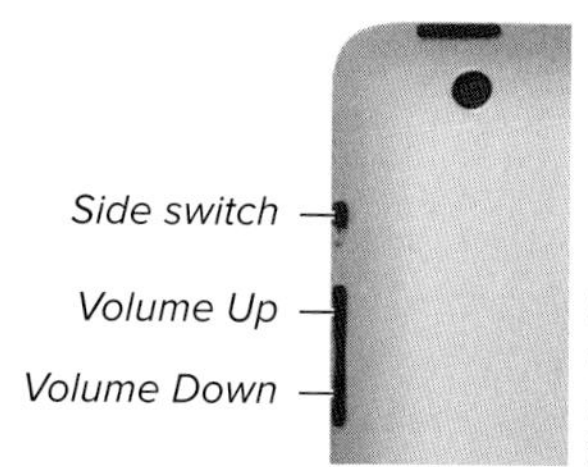

A Use these controls to increase, decrease, or mute the sound.

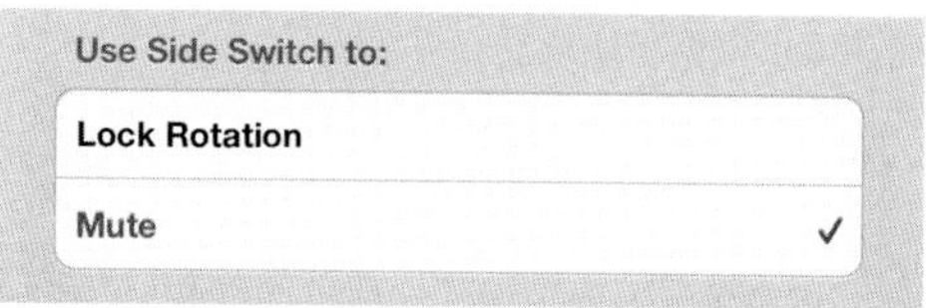

B Out of the box, the iPad's side switch is a Mute button, but you may find it to be more useful as a Lock Rotation button, which was its default behavior on the original iPad.

Alert Sounds

Tap Settings > General > Sounds to open the Sounds screen **C**, where you can set your iPad to play a sound for certain system events: email, messages, tweets, reminders, appointments, keyboard clicks, and more.

To let the volume buttons adjust the alert volume, turn on Change with Buttons. To adjust the alert volume, drag the slider (or, if Change with Buttons is turned on, use the volume buttons on the side of the iPad).

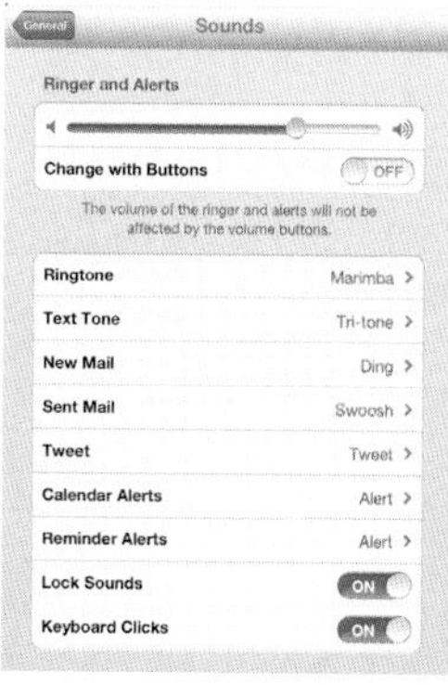

C The Sounds screen lets you toggle or change specific audio alerts.

To increase the volume:

- Press the Volume Up button.

  To raise the volume quickly, press and hold for a second or two.

TIP To limit the maximum volume (if you're worried about hearing loss), tap Settings > Music > Volume Limit.

To decrease the volume:

- Press the Volume Down button.

TIP You can also change the volume by using the audio playback controls: Double-click the Home button to show the multitasking bar at the bottom of the screen, flick left to right, and then drag the volume slider. (If your iPad is locked, the playback controls appear at the top of the screen when you double-click Home.)

To mute the sound:

- Press and hold the Volume Down button for a second or two.

  or

  Slide the side switch down. (This option is available only if you've set the side switch to Mute; to do so, tap Settings > General.)

  or

  Double-click the Home button to show the multitasking bar at the bottom of the screen, flick left to right, and then tap the speaker icon. (This option is available only if you've set the side switch to Lock Rotation; to do so, tap Settings > General.)

TIP Muting suppresses only certain sounds. Alerts, notifications, sound effects, and game audio are muted. Media playback (such as music, podcasts, movies, videos, and TV shows) *isn't* muted.

Earphones and Speakers

The iPad doesn't come with earphones, but it does have a headphone jack on its top-left edge. More precisely, it has a standard 3.5mm stereo headphone minijack. You can plug in any earphones or headsets that come with the 3.5mm miniplug (including the earphones that come with iPhones and iPods). Push the plug firmly into the jack so that it connects fully.

Certain audio accessories, like stereo-audio docks and external speakers, plug into the iPad's dock connector (the flat port on the iPad's bottom edge) or connect wirelessly via Bluetooth. To pair wireless speakers with your iPad, tap Settings > General > Bluetooth > On. After the iPad finds and lists your accessory, tap its name; then, if required, type a passkey (which you'll find in the gadget's manual).

The iPad's built-in speaker—the perforated area on the back near the dock connector—is silenced when you use earphones or external speakers.

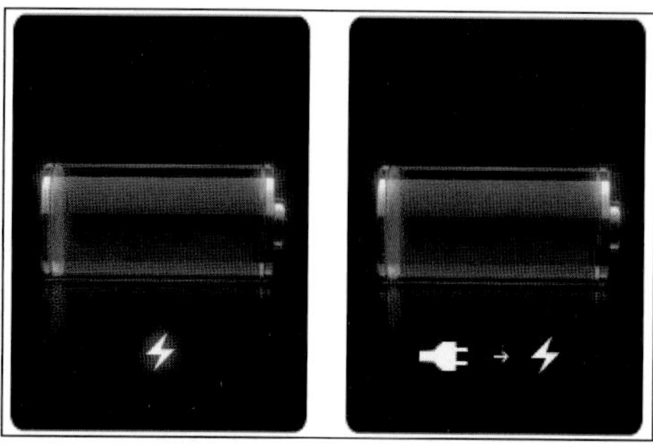

Ⓐ If one of these screens appears, keep your iPad connected and charging.

Ⓑ If *Not Charging* appears in the status bar, you must charge your iPad from a power outlet.

Charging the Battery

A drained iPad lacks sufficient power to show the Home screen. You may have to charge it for more than 2 minutes before it shows the *Charging. Please Wait* screen and for more than 10 minutes before it can show the Home screen Ⓐ.

A few charging tips:

- Charge your iPad by using only the Apple iPad 10W USB Power Adapter that came with your iPad (or that you bought separately from Apple). Don't use an Apple USB Power Adapter or an adapter that came with an iPhone/iPod; these adapters look compatible, but their power output is too small to charge an iPad.
- The USB cable that came with your iPad is interchangeable with an iPhone/iPod USB cable.
- In most cases, you must charge your iPad from a power outlet rather than by connecting it to your computer's USB port, as you would do to charge an iPhone or iPod. Some newer computers (such as late-model iMacs) *can* charge an iPad via USB cable, but most computers' USB ports lack the necessary power. To determine whether your computer has enough juice, connect your iPad to it via USB cable. When a connected iPad isn't charging, the notification *Not Charging* appears next to the battery icon in the status bar at the top of the screen Ⓑ.

continues on next page

- The battery icon in the status bar shows the battery level or charging status. To turn on the battery percentage indicator, tap Settings > General > Usage > Battery Percentage. When you connect your iPad to power or wake it from sleep, the battery and charge indicators can fluctuate for a few seconds before stabilizing. It's not unusual for the battery-level reading to show *99%* even when the iPad is fully charged.
- Battery life and charge cycles vary by use and settings. A properly maintained battery should deliver up to 1,000 charge cycles and retain 80 percent or more of its original capacity over a typical 5-year life span.

Be a Power Miser

When you're not using your iPad, put it to sleep to conserve power (by pressing the Sleep/Wake button). When you're using it, the battery drains more slowly if you:

- Dim the screen brightness (tap Settings > Brightness & Wallpaper).
- Turn off Wi-Fi, cellular, VPN, and Bluetooth connections when you're not using them (see Chapter 3).
- Turn off or minimize the use of Location Services (tap Settings > Location Services).
- Turn off unused iCloud services (tap Settings > iCloud).
- Turn off or reduce notifications (tap Settings > Notifications).
- Turn off push (tap Settings > Mail, Contacts, Calendars > Fetch New Data > Push > Off).
- Fetch new data manually (tap Settings > Mail, Contacts, Calendars > Fetch New Data > Manually).

Despite widespread tips to the contrary, closing apps in the multitasking bar does little to conserve power or memory. For technical details, see http://speirs.org/blog/2012/1/2/misconceptions-about-ios-multitasking.html.

For more tips on minimizing power consumption and extending battery life, see www.apple.com/batteries/ipad.html.

Liquid Contact Indicators

Don't get any moisture in your iPad's openings. Should the iPad ever need service, the Apple technician will determine whether it's been in contact with liquid by looking at the bottom of the headphone jack and in the dock connector port. Both places have *liquid contact indicators* (LCIs) that turn pink and stay pink on contact with liquid—and if they do, your warranty goes poof!

Cleaning the Screen

The Pad's glass touchscreen has a special coating that does its best to repel fingerprints, but eventually, it will accumulate oils, glazed sugar, sunscreen, or whatever else you have on your hands. To clean the screen, wipe it gently with a soft, lint-free cloth—the same kind that you use to clean eyeglasses or camera lenses.

To clean the rest of the iPad, unplug it from any docks or USB cables and then turn it off. (Press and hold the Sleep/Wake button until a red slider appears; then drag the slider.) You can use a cloth that's dampened lightly with water, but never use window cleaners, household cleaners, anything from a spray can, alcohol- or ammonia-based cleansers, solvents, or abrasives.

Securing Your iPad

You can use the iPad's security features to protect your data from co-workers, thieves, cops, spouses, lawyers, busybodies, and governments.

Passcodes

You can set up a security passcode that you must enter each time you power on or wake your iPad (see "Powering On and Off" earlier in this chapter). Setting a passcode turns on *data protection,* which uses the passcode as the key to encrypt your data. The message *Data protection is enabled* at the bottom of the Passcode Lock screen lets you know that your data is encrypted.

The iPad's built-in apps use data encryption (Mail, for example, encrypts your messages and attachments), but third-party apps may or may not use it.

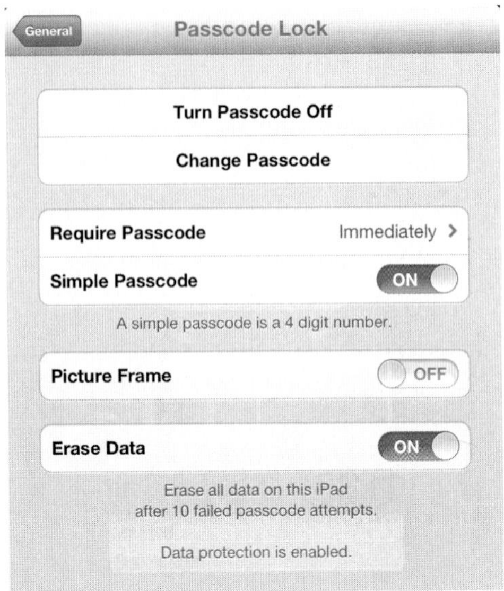

A The Passcode Lock screen lets you set your passcode and fine-tune security options.

To set a passcode:

1. Tap Settings > General > Passcode Lock to open the Passcode Lock screen **A**.
2. Choose any of the following options:
   - **Turn Passcode On.** Type a four-digit passcode and then retype it to verify it. From now on, your iPad makes you type the passcode to unlock it or to change or turn off the passcode.
   - **Turn Passcode Off.** Turn off the passcode.
   - **Change Passcode.** Change an existing passcode.

Forgotten Passcodes

You can't decrypt your data without the key. If Erase Data is turned off, you *can* keep entering different passcodes until you hit the right one. After a few wrong guesses, however, the iPad disables itself—first for 1 minute, then 5 minutes, then 15 minutes, then 60 minutes—before letting you guess again. Statistically, you'd have to enter thousands of guesses for years before you stumbled on the right passcode.

If Erase Data is turned on, you get ten free guesses until your data is gone forever and you must restore the iPad software.

- **Require Passcode.** Select how long your iPad will wait after being locked before it requires your passcode to be unlocked again. By default, the passcode is required immediately, which is secure but inconvenient if you've set a short Auto-Lock time (by tapping Settings > General > Auto-Lock).
- **Simple Passcode.** A simple passcode is a four-digit number. For added security, turn off Simple Passcode, and use a longer passcode with a combination of numbers, letters, punctuation, and special characters.
- **Picture Frame.** Tap Settings > Picture Frame to remove the Picture Frame button from the Lock screen.
- **Erase Data.** For real peace of mind, you can direct your iPad to erase all your data after ten failed passcode attempts. After the tenth mistyped passcode, all settings are reset, and the iPad erases all your information and media by removing the encryption key.

Find My iPad

You can use Find My iPad to track down a lost or stolen iPad by showing its approximate location on a map, provided that the missing iPad is turned on and connected to a Wi-Fi or cellular network. You must set up Find My iPad *before* you lose your iPad.

To find your iPad, you can sign in to https://www.icloud.com from any Web browser on a Mac or Windows PC, or use the Find My iPhone app on an iPhone, an iPod touch, or another iPad. You can download Find My iPhone for free from the App Store. (This app, despite its name, finds iPads as well as iPhones.)

TIP To use Find My iPad, you need an iCloud account. If you didn't create one when you first set up your iPad, tap Settings > iCloud and then create an account.

To set up Find My iPad:

1. Tap Settings > iCloud.
2. If necessary, sign in to iCloud.
3. On the iCloud screen, turn on Find My iPad.
4. In the permission box that appears, tap Allow.
5. Tap Home > Settings > General > Location Services > On.

   This service can show your iPad's location on a map.

To find a missing iPad:

1. On a Mac or Windows PC, open a Web browser, go to https://www.icloud.com, sign in to iCloud, and then click the Find My iPhone icon on the main page.

   or

   On an iPhone, iPod touch, or iPad, open the Find My iPhone app and then sign in to iCloud.

   In either case, a map appears, showing your iPad's location **B**.

2. (Optional) Click or tap ⓘ next to the iPad icon on the map and then choose an option in the pop-up box or screen:

   - Send a message (such as "Please return my iPad" or "Call 415-555-1234").
   - Play a sound at full volume for 2 minutes (handy if you've misplaced your iPad under a pillow).
   - Lock your iPad, and create a four-digit passcode (if you haven't set one previously).
   - Wipe your iPad's contents entirely, erasing sensitive data and restoring the iPad to its factory settings.

B If you've enabled Find My iPad for multiple devices, choose a specific device in the My Devices list.

Restrictions

If you lend your iPad to guests or kids, tap Settings > General > Restrictions > Enable Restrictions to set up access rules **C**. You must set a passcode to use this feature. You can block anyone who doesn't know your passcode from using specific apps (Safari, YouTube, iTunes, and so on), making video calls on FaceTime, installing or deleting apps, taking photos, dictating text, mapping whereabouts, creating or editing accounts, playing multiplayer games, listening to naughty lyrics, and more.

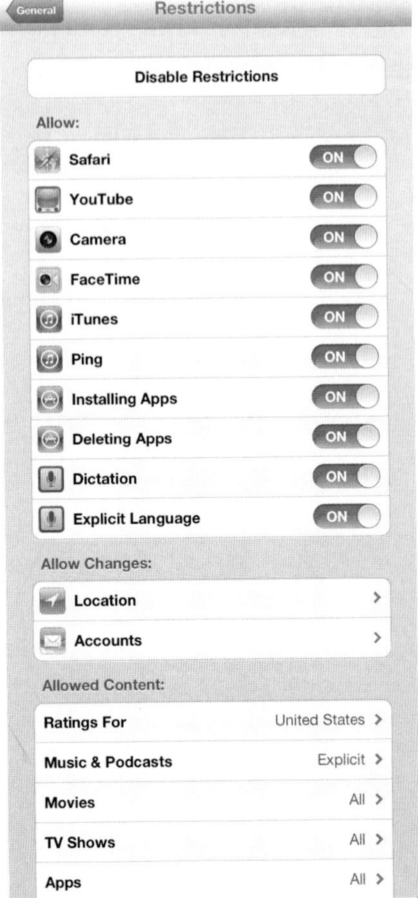

C You can toggle restrictions independently. The icons of restricted apps are removed from the Home screen.

2

Working with Text

The iPad isn't all scrolling, dragging, and zooming; it also offers an onscreen keyboard and other tools for working with text. This chapter shows you how to:

- Use the onscreen keyboard
- Dictate text
- Type with your thumbs
- Add a wireless keyboard
- Type in other languages
- Cut, copy, and paste text
- Define words by using the built-in dictionary
- Search your iPad
- Print from your iPad

In This Chapter

Using the Onscreen Keyboard

An onscreen keyboard pops up automatically when you tap any area that accepts text **A**. Use the keyboard to type notes, mail, messages, Web addresses, passwords, search terms, contact information, or any other text.

Typing is straightforward: Tap a character to make it appear in the editing area. The target key turns a darker gray when you tap it.

TIP The fake bumps on the F and J keys are a jokey effect for touch-typists, who use real bumps to position their hands on physical keyboards without looking at the keys.

The onscreen keyboard has much in common with its physical counterpart, plus a few tricks:

- **Keyboard orientation.** The keyboard reorients for portrait (tall) and landscape (wide) views. The latter view is roomier for typing. For details, see "Changing Screen Orientation" in Chapter 1.
- **Uppercase letters.** To type an uppercase letter, tap the Shift key ⇧. This key turns blue when it's active and then back to gray after you type a letter.
- **Deleting characters.** To delete the last character that you typed, tap the Backspace key. To delete multiple characters quickly, touch and hold the Backspace key. If you hold it down for more than a few seconds, it deletes entire words.
- **Hiding the keyboard.** To hide the keyboard, tap the Keyboard key, or tap off an editable area.

A The iPad offers alphabetic, numbers-and-punctuation, and symbols keyboards, which you can switch among as you type.

B Touch and hold a key to see whether it offers additional letters or symbols. The E key, for example, lets you type not only the standard e, but also ë, é, è, ê, and other diacriticals.

- **Accents and diacritical marks.** You can touch and hold certain keys to see variants of their characters in a pop-up box **B**. Slide your finger to the target character in the box and then lift your finger to type it.
- **Apostrophes and quotes.** To type an apostrophe (single quote), which isn't on the alphabetic keyboard, touch the comma key (,) and then slide your finger up to insert the apostrophe. To type a double quote, do the same action on the period key (.).
- **Switching keyboards.** In the alphabetic keyboard, tap the **.?123** key to see numbers and most punctuation; within that layout, tap the #+= key to see less-common symbols, tap **123** to return to the numbers-and-punctuation layout, or tap **ABC** to return to the alphabetic keys.
- **Switching keyboards momentarily.** You can quickly type a character in a different keyboard without switching away from the current one. On the alphabetic keyboard, for example, touch and hold the **.?123** key; still touching the screen, slide your finger up to the numeric character you want; and then lift your finger. Characters are typed only when you lift your finger.
- **Fat fingers.** If you have your finger on the wrong key but haven't lifted it from the screen yet, slide it over to the correct one and then lift.
- **Context-sensitive Return key.** In ordinary text, Return moves from one line to the next. It changes to Go when you type a Web address in Safari, Join when you type a Wi-Fi password, and Search when you type in a search box.

continues on next page

- **Web addresses.** When you type a Web address (URL) in Safari, the iPad's Web browser, the keyboard includes keys for commonly used characters. The spacebar is replaced by colon, slash, underscore, hyphen, and .com keys. (Spaces aren't allowed in URLs.) Press and hold the .com key to get your choice of .net, .org, .edu, and other top-level domains **C**, depending on what country or region you've set your iPad for.
- **Specialized keyboards.** Some apps offer specialized keyboards for specific tasks. Apple's Numbers app, for example, has a keyboard adapted for entering spreadsheet formulas **D**.

C When you're typing a Web address in Safari, touch and hold the .com key to type a different suffix.

D This app-specific keyboard in Numbers is designed for typing spreadsheet formulas.

Dictating Text

On the iPad 3 or later, you can dictate text instead of typing on the onscreen keyboard. To dictate, you must be connected to the Internet.

To turn on dictation, tap Settings > General > Keyboard > Dictation.

To dictate, tap 🎙 on the keyboard and then speak **E**. When you're finished, tap 🎙. To add more text, tap 🎙 again and then continue speaking. (The 🎙 key won't appear if you're not online.)

E Dictation on the iPad.

Try dictating a message in Mail or a note in Notes. To enter punctuation, say the punctuation mark. Suppose that you want to dictate "Without me, you're nothing." Say this:

Without me comma you're nothing period

To start a new paragraph, say "new paragraph." To type *5* rather than *five,* say "numeral five." Saying more than one digit in a row also produces numerals: Saying "four five" types *45,* not *four five.*

Dictation works in most places that you can enter text by using the keyboard. The iPad hears you through its built-in microphone (the small hole in the top-center edge); as an alternative, you can use an audio accessory such as a wireless headset. If you want to disable dictation, tap Settings > General > Restrictions > Dictation.

At this writing, dictation is available in English (Australian, British, and American dialects), French, German, and Japanese. To dictate in a supported language, add an international keyboard for that language (see "Using International Keyboards" later in this chapter).

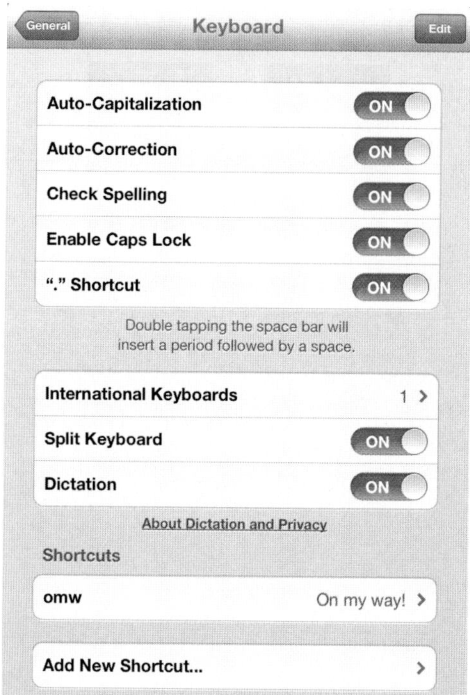

A After you get the hang of typing on the onscreen keyboard, you'll know whether a particular typing option is helpful or irritating.

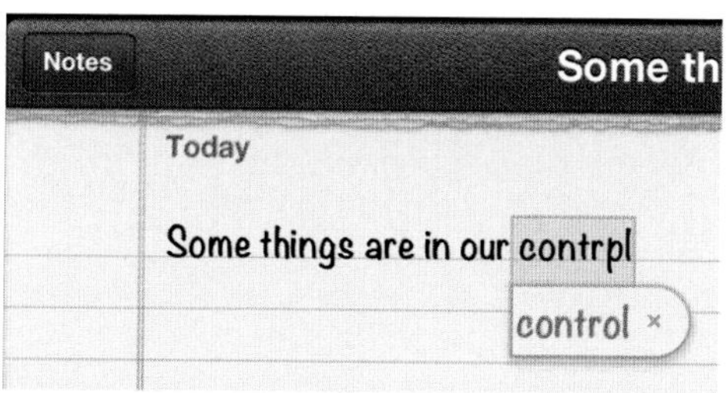

B Auto-Correction in action.

Setting Typing Options

The onscreen keyboard has several built-in shortcuts and tricks that you can turn on or off. Tap Settings > General > Keyboard and then toggle the following settings **A**:

- **Auto-Capitalization.** This setting automatically capitalizes the first letter after a period.
- **Auto-Correction.** As you type, the iPad can automatically suggest corrections for typos and spelling errors in a little pop-up box **B**. To accept a suggestion, type a space, punctuation mark, or Return character. To reject it, finish typing the word and then tap × in the pop-up box. Missing apostrophes in contractions are also fixed; type **cant** or **youll**, and it's corrected to *can't* or *you'll*. The built-in keyboard dictionary recognizes proper nouns and often makes needless suggestions, but if you reject a word a few times, it's added to the dictionary. (To reset the keyboard dictionary to its original state, tap Settings > General > Reset > Reset Keyboard Dictionary.)

TIP If you stare at the keyboard (not the text) as you type, you won't notice autocorrections until after they're made. To make Auto-Correction announce its suggestions aloud, tap Settings > General > Accessibility > Speak Auto-Text.

continues on next page

- **Check Spelling.** This setting flags misspelled words with a red underline. Tap the flagged word to see replacement options **C**.
- **Enable Caps Lock.** This setting switches to typing UPPERCASE LETTERS for a while.

TIP You can also enable caps lock by double-tapping the Shift key ⇧. The key turns blue, and all letters that you type are uppercase until you tap the Shift key again to turn off caps lock.

- **"." Shortcut.** Double-tap the spacebar at the end of a sentence to end it with a period, move one space to the right, and start the next sentence with an uppercase letter.

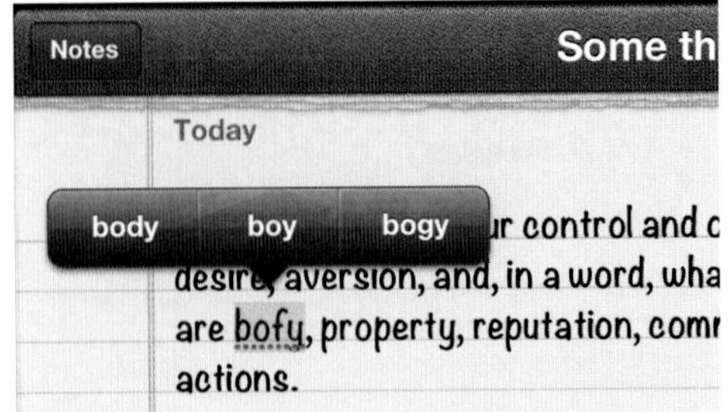

C Tap one of the alternative spellings to replace the misspelled word. If the word that you want doesn't appear, just retype it.

Shortcuts

The Shortcuts feature saves you time and typing by expanding short bits of typed text into longer words, phrases, or sentences. (Microsoft Word users know this feature as AutoCorrect.) You can tell Shortcuts that when you type **syt**, for example, it should automatically expand that to *See you tomorrow* **D**. Shortcuts comes with a sample shortcut: **omw** expands to *On my way!*

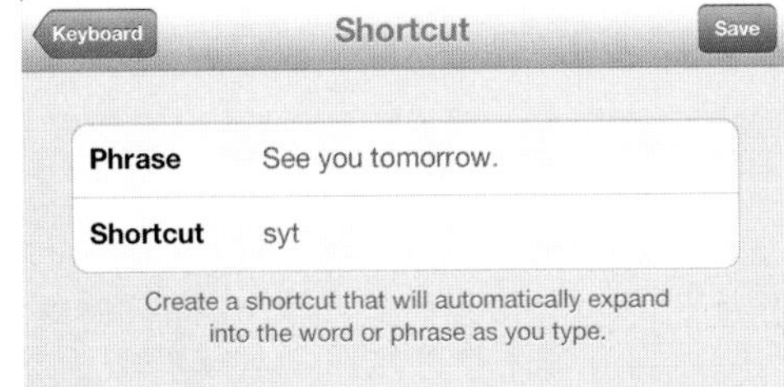

D A shortcut.

To create a new shortcut, follow these steps:

1. Tap Settings > General > Keyboard > Add New Shortcut **A**.
2. In the Phrase field, type the full word or words that you want to appear when you type the shortcut, such as *See you tomorrow.*
3. In the Shortcut field, type the characters that you want Shortcuts to autoexpand, such as **syt**.
4. Tap the Save button in the top-right corner.

The Shortcut field is optional. If you leave it blank, what you type in the Phrase field is added to the keyboard dictionary and won't be autocorrected or replaced as a misspelling in the future.

To edit a shortcut, tap Settings > General > Keyboard. To delete a shortcut, flick left or right on its entry and then tap Delete.

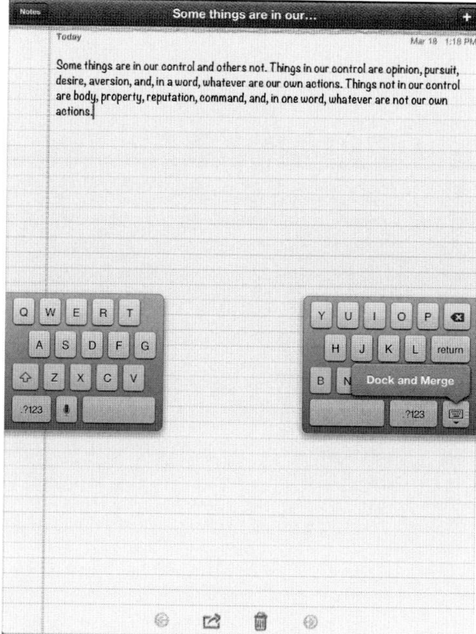

A A split keyboard, docked midscreen.

Splitting and Moving the Keyboard

If you're holding your iPad, versus resting it on a flat surface, you may prefer to type with your thumbs, the way you do on a smartphone. You can split the keyboard in half, positioning the keys much closer to your thumbs, and optionally move the keyboard to the middle of the screen **A**. A split keyboard works in portrait (tall) and landscape (wide) orientations.

To turn keyboard splitting on or off:

- Tap Settings > General > Keyboard > Split Keyboard.

To split the keyboard:

- Place a finger on each half of the keyboard and then drag or flick your fingers in opposite directions.

  or

  Touch and hold the Keyboard key ⌨, slide your finger to Split, and then lift your finger.

To rejoin a split keyboard:

- Place a finger on each half of the keyboard and then drag or flick your fingers toward the middle of the screen.

To move the keyboard to midscreen:

- Touch and hold the Keyboard key ⌨, slide your finger to Undock, and then lift your finger.

To return the keyboard to the bottom of the screen:

- Touch and hold the Keyboard key ⌨, slide your finger to Dock, and then lift your finger.

To return to a normal keyboard:

- Touch and hold the Keyboard key ⌨, slide your finger to Dock and Merge, and then lift your finger.

Using a Wireless Keyboard

If you type a lot of text, work with large documents, or just don't like typing on glass, you can use a wireless keyboard with your iPad. Wireless keyboards use Bluetooth technology to establish a wireless handshake with your iPad. Before you can use a Bluetooth keyboard, you must make it discoverable and then pair it with your iPad; the keyboard will come with instructions.

After pairing, the keyboard autoconnects whenever it's within range (up to 33 feet) of your iPad.

TIP See also "Using Bluetooth Devices" in Chapter 3.

Apple Wireless Keyboard

The Apple Wireless Keyboard **A** is available in multiple languages and is the most popular iPad-compatible Bluetooth keyboard. You can buy it (or an iPad-compatible keyboard from another manufacturer) from tech retailers, Apple retail stores, the online Apple Store (http://store.apple.com), or online stores like Amazon.com.

Before you pair an Apple Wireless Keyboard, press the power button to turn the keyboard on and make it discoverable.

A Apple Wireless Keyboard.

To pair a Bluetooth keyboard with an iPad:

1. Follow the instructions that came with the keyboard to make it discoverable.
2. Tap Settings > General > Bluetooth > On.

   When you turn on Bluetooth, the iPad finds nearby discoverable devices and lists them in the Devices list.
3. Tap the keyboard in the Devices list and then type the requested passkey or PIN (located in the keyboard manual) to complete the pairing.

   To confirm the pairing, the keyboard name appears on the Bluetooth screen, and a white Bluetooth icon ✱ appears in the status bar at the top of the screen.

TIP When a physical keyboard is paired, the onscreen keyboard doesn't appear when you tap in a text field.

TIP You can pair only one wireless keyboard at a time. To pair a different keyboard, you must first unpair the current one.

To go back to using the onscreen keyboard:

- Tap Settings > General > Bluetooth > Off.

  or

  Turn off the keyboard.

  or

  Press the Eject key on the keyboard.

  or

  Move the iPad out of range of the keyboard.

To unpair a wireless keyboard from an iPad:

1. Tap Settings > General > Bluetooth.
2. Tap next to the keyboard name.
3. Tap Forget This Device.

Using International Keyboards

If you communicate in more than one language, you can add keyboards to type in Spanish, Italian, French, German, Chinese, Japanese, Russian, and many more. You can switch keyboards at any time.

To add an international keyboard:

1. Tap Settings > General > International > Keyboards > Add New Keyboard **A**.
2. Tap a keyboard language.

   The keyboard is added to your list of keyboards, which you can view by tapping Settings > General> Keyboard > International Keyboard > Keyboards **B**.
3. To change the keyboard layout, tap the language name in the list of keyboards and then tap a layout **C**.
4. If you're going to use an external (physical) keyboard, you can select a hardware layout too.

A Language variants are listed by country, region, or dialect—German (Germany) or German (Switzerland), for example. The Emoji keyboard adds smiley faces and other picture characters to text.

B Your personal list of keyboard languages.

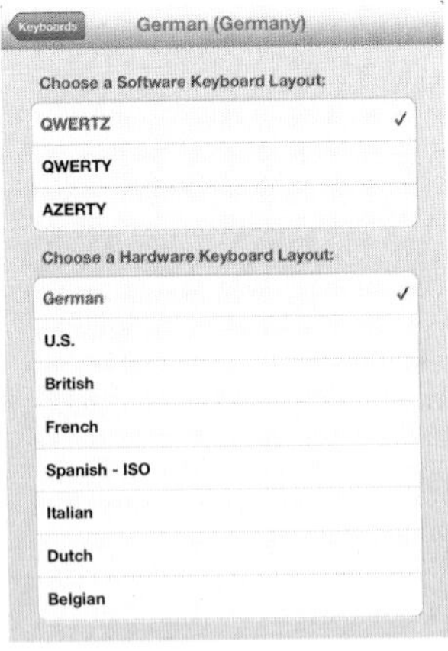

C Depending on the language, you can use QWERTY, AZERTY, QWERTZ, or other keyboard layouts, including layouts for non-Western character sets.

D Go to the globe when you want to switch keyboard languages.

E You can reorder or delete keyboards.

To switch keyboards:

- Tap the Globe key 🌐 repeatedly to cycle through your keyboards. Stop when the name of the desired keyboard flashes on the spacebar.

  or

  Touch and hold the Globe key 🌐, slide your finger to name of the desired keyboard, and then lift your finger **D**.

TIP The Globe key appears only if you've added multiple keyboards.

To edit your keyboards list:

1. Tap Settings > General > International > Keyboards.
2. Tap the Edit button above the Keyboards list.
3. To reorder the keyboards **E**, drag ≡ next to a keyboard up or down.
4. To delete a keyboard, tap ⊖ next to the target keyboard and then tap Delete.
5. Tap Done.

Chinese Handwriting

The iPad offers several languages that use non-Western (non-Latin) character sets, including Arabic, Japanese, and Chinese. When you choose Chinese (Simplified) Handwriting or Chinese (Traditional) Handwriting, you can draw Chinese characters on the keyboard's touchpad area with your finger .

As you draw the character strokes, you're offered a list of matching characters to choose among, with the closest match at the top **F**. When you choose a character, its likely follow-on characters appear in the list as additional choices. You can create some complex characters by drawing two or more component characters in sequence.

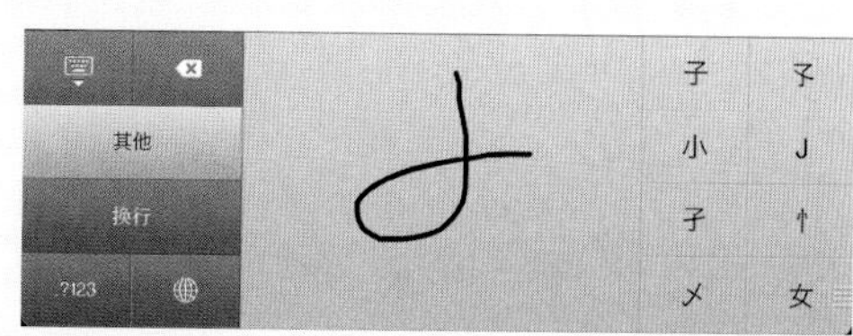

F Drawing Chinese characters.

Selecting and Editing Text

The basic text-editing operations are

- **Select.** Highlights text to edit, cut, copy, or format.
- **Cut and paste.** Removes (cuts) content and places it in the Clipboard so that it can be moved (pasted) elsewhere. Cutting deletes the content from its original location.
- **Copy and paste.** Copies content to the Clipboard so that it can be duplicated (pasted) elsewhere. Copying leaves the original content intact—that is, nothing visible happens.

TIP The select, cut, copy, and paste operations apply not only to text, but also to other objects—photos, images, videos, shapes, tables, charts, and so on—that are used in various apps.

You can select any portion of text within an editable area and then edit it by typing or by using the standard cut, copy, and paste operations.

The Clipboard

The Clipboard is the invisible area of memory where the iPad stores cut or copied content until it's overwritten when you cut or copy something else. This scheme lets you paste the same thing multiple times in different places. You can transfer content from one app to another, provided that the second app can read content generated by the first.

Note that you can't paste something that you've deleted (as opposed to cut), because the iPad doesn't place the deleted item in the Clipboard.

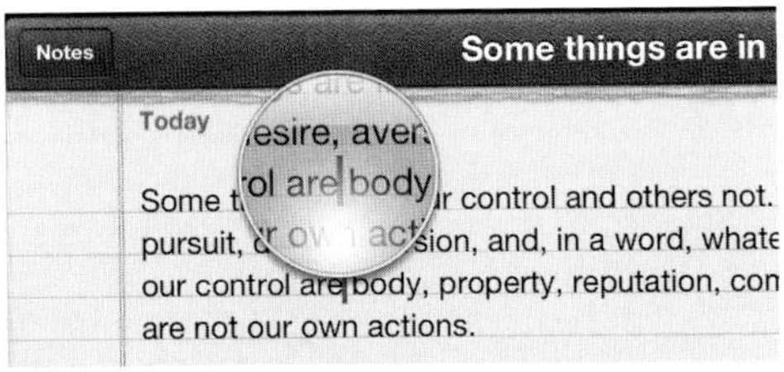

A An onscreen magnifying glass helps you position the insertion point where you need it to be.

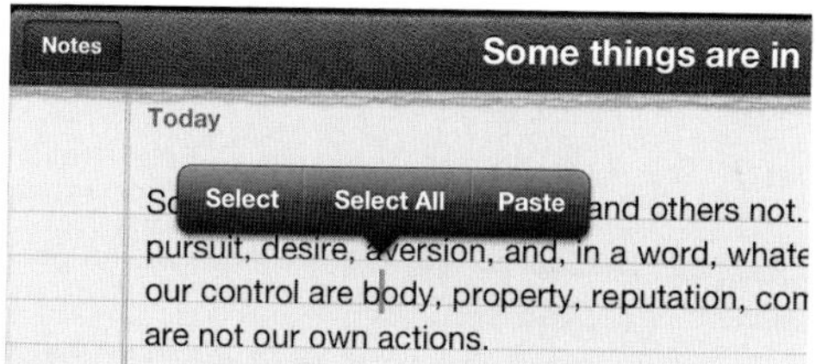

B Choose Select or Select All to select text quickly.

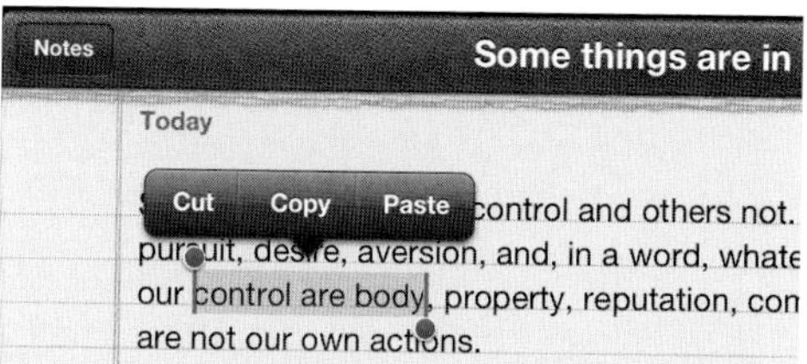

C The editing pop-up menu appears when you select text or change the selection by dragging the blue drag points.

Selecting and editing text can work differently, depending on which app you're using. In most cases, these rules apply:

- When you tap text in an editable area, a blinking insertion point indicates where new text will appear when you type or paste.
- To move the insertion point, touch and hold near where you want to place it until a magnifying glass appears. Drag over the text to the new position and then lift your finger **A**.
- To select a word, double-tap it. To select a paragraph, tap it quickly four times. Alternatively, double-tap a word and then, without lifting your finger, drag to encompass the range that you want to select, including whole or partial words and paragraphs.
- To open the selection pop-up menu, tap once in an editable area and then tap again in the same place. The Select command selects the current word. The Select All command selects all the text in the field or the document **B**.
- To extend or shorten the range of selected text, drag the blue drag points to encompass the characters or paragraphs that you want to select.
- To cut or copy text, select a range of text and then tap Cut or Copy. To paste text, move the insertion point (or select some text to replace) and then tap Paste **C**.

TIP **In read-only areas—such as in incoming emails and Web pages—the Cut and Paste commands aren't available. (The Notes app is the handiest place to paste text that you copy from read-only areas.)**

continues on next page

- If you make a mistake, tap the **.?123** key and then tap **undo** on the numbers keyboard. Alternatively, give your iPad a quick shake to bring up the Undo/Redo box **D**.

TIP Shaking front to back works better than shaking side to side.

- If you select a word, the Suggest command appears in the pop-up menu. (If you don't see it, tap ▶ in the menu.) Tap Suggest if you want to replace the word with an alternative spelling **E**. In some cases, Suggest has no suggestions.

TIP Apps have no manual Save command. Changes are saved automatically about every 30 seconds, or when you switch away from or close the app.

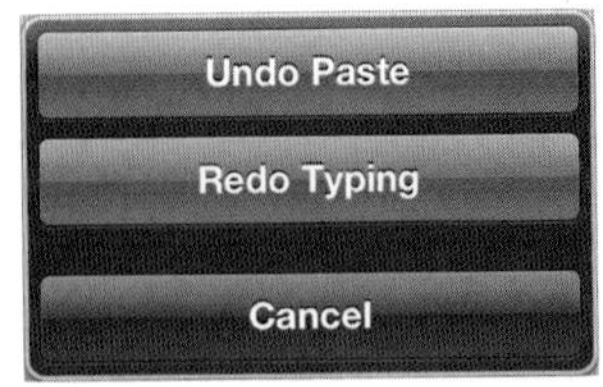

D A shake brings up the Undo/Redo box in some apps. (Notes is shown here.)

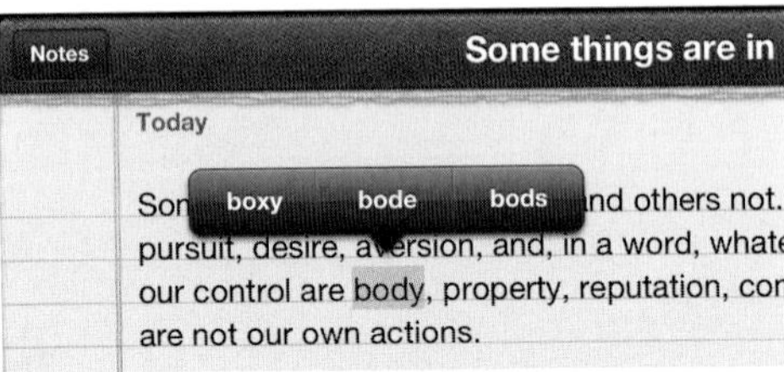

E The Suggest command offers a few alternative words. If you see the word that you meant to type, tap it to replace the selected word.

Defining Words

If you select a word, compound word, or proper noun, the Define command appears in a pop-up menu. (If you don't see it, tap ▶ in the menu.) This command accesses the iPad's built-in dictionary, which works with most text-oriented apps, such as Notes, Safari, and Mail. Tap Define to see the selected word's definition in a pop-up box **F**. Flick up or down the box to see the word forms (noun, verb, and so on), phrases, derivatives, and origin.

The dictionary recognizes proper nouns, so you'll get different definitions depending on whether you've selected *Boulder* (a city in Colorado) or *boulder* (a large rock).

To dismiss the dictionary, tap off the pop-up box.

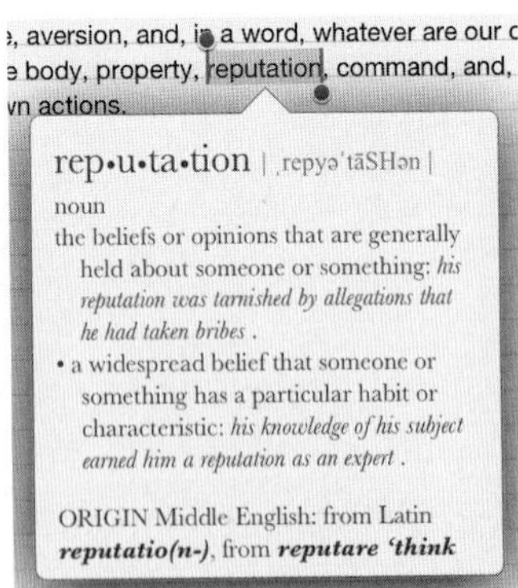

rep•u•ta•tion
noun
the beliefs or opinions that are generally held about someone or something: his reputation was tarnished by allegations that he had taken bribes.
• a widespread belief that someone or something has a particular habit or characteristic: his knowledge of his subject earned him a reputation as an expert.
ORIGIN Middle English: from Latin reputatio(n-), from reputare 'think

F Viewing a definition.

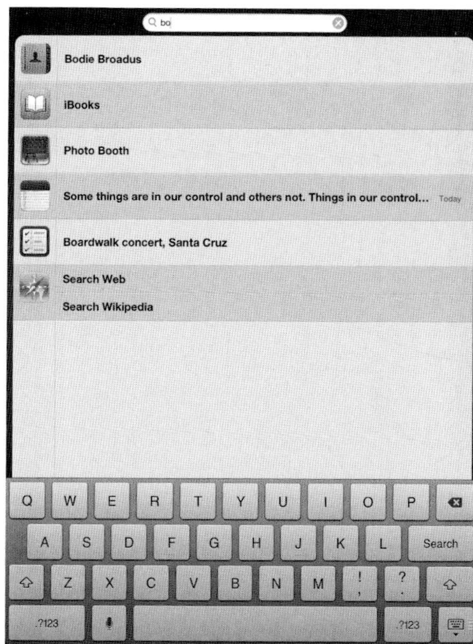

A Icons to the left of the search results indicate which apps the results are from.

Searching Your iPad

If your iPad is loaded with gigabytes of stuff—contacts, apps, events, music, videos, notes, email, reminders, messages, and so on—you often can find things faster by using the built-in search tool, called *Spotlight,* than by tapping around looking for something. Spotlight lets you scan your iPad for words, apps, names, titles, addresses, phrases, and more.

TIP For the Mail app, Spotlight searches the To, From, and Subject fields of email, but not the body text of messages. For the Messages app, names and text of messages are searched.

To search your iPad:

1. If you're on your first Home screen, press the Home button.

   or

   On any home screen, flick left to right repeatedly until you *pass* the first Home screen.

   The Spotlight screen appears.

2. In the Search field, type the text that you're looking for **A**.

   As you type, items that match your text are listed. The results list narrows as you type more characters. To restart the search, tap ⊗ in the Search field.

3. Tap an item in the results list to open it.

   The options at the bottom of the list let you send your search to the Web or to Wikipedia.

TIP To choose which apps are searched and the order they're searched in, tap Settings > General > Spotlight Search.

Printing from Your iPad

You have two ways to print from your iPad:

- **Apps.** The App Store offers many utility programs that provide iPad-based printing by getting a document from an app and then sending it to a printer—either directly to a shared network printer or wirelessly via a helper program that you install on your computer. Open App Store and then type **print** in the Search box. To find a suitable app, read the description and the customer ratings and reviews. Buy it, install it, and then follow the app's instructions for printing. (The best printing apps are *not* free.) Be sure to buy an app that lets you print to all printers, not only AirPrint printers.
- **AirPrint.** To print wirelessly by using Apple's AirPrint technology, you must buy an AirPrint-compatible printer—an expensive option but easier to use because AirPrint is baked into the iPad. An AirPrint printer doesn't need additional printer software or a separate app; it just needs to be connected to the same Wi-Fi network as your iPad. AirPrint works with Mail, Photos, Camera, Safari, iBooks (PDF files), Notes, and Maps. Other apps from the App Store, like iWork (Numbers, Pages, and Keynote) and Evernote, also let you print.

  To print, open the document, tap [share icon] or [reply icon] or [wrench icon] (depending on the app), set the printer options **A**, and then tap Print. To see and manage your print jobs, double-click the Home button while a document is printing and then tap Print Center in the multitasking bar at the bottom of the screen.

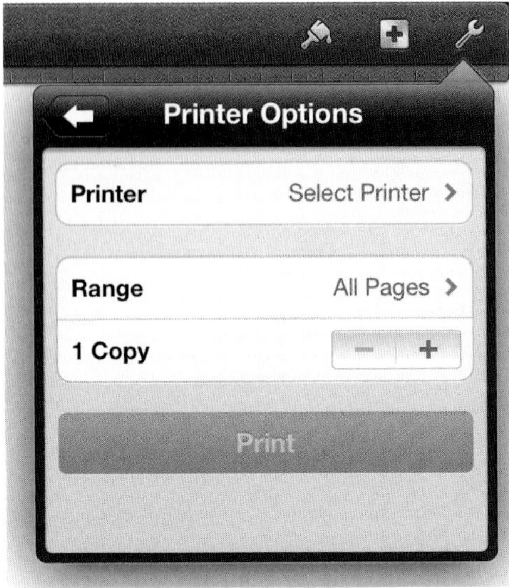

A The Printer Options box lets you select a printer, choose the pages you want to print, and specify the number of copies.

Online and Wireless Connections

Every iPad can access the Internet over a Wi-Fi connection. You can jump online from a wireless network at home, work, or school, or from a public Wi-Fi hotspot at a library, café, or airport.

The costlier Wi-Fi+4G iPads (or Wi-Fi+3G, for older models) can also connect to the Internet through a cellular network—the same network that you use to make mobile phone calls. In the United States, for example, you can use AT&T or Verizon cellular service, depending on which 4G/3G iPad model you bought.

Unlike Wi-Fi, 4G/3G doesn't anchor you to a stationary network. You can use the Internet anywhere you can make a mobile phone call (including a moving vehicle). When you have a choice, stick with Wi-Fi; it's likely to be faster and doesn't incur carrier charges against your data plan's monthly limit.

This chapter also covers the iPad's other wireless features: hotspots, Bluetooth, VPNs (virtual private networks), and more.

In This Chapter

Making Wi-Fi Connections

Wi-Fi—also known by its less-catchy technical name, *IEEE 802.11*—is the same technology that laptop computers and handheld gadgets use to get online at high speed. After your iPad is connected to a Wi-Fi network, you can browse the Web, send and receive email, view maps, and do other tasks that require an Internet connection. Wi-Fi also lets you interact with other devices and computers on the same network. You can control iTunes music playback on your computer, control movie playback on an Apple TV, or play a game against another iPad user, for example.

When your iPad needs an Internet connection, such as when you browse to a Web site in Safari, it automatically scans for active Wi-Fi networks within range and then pops open a box listing them **A**. Tap the name of a network that you want to join. If the network is secured, type its password and then tap Join. When your iPad is joined to a Wi-Fi network, the Wi-Fi icon in the status bar at the top of the screen shows the signal strength. The more bars, the stronger the signal.

TIP If you join a public, unsecured Wi-Fi network, it's easy for the network owner or nearby intruders to collect the unencrypted data (passwords, credit-card numbers, Web addresses, and so on) flowing between your iPad and the wireless router. Don't shop, bank, or pay bills on such networks. If you have no choice, use a VPN service like WiTopia (https://www.witopia.net).

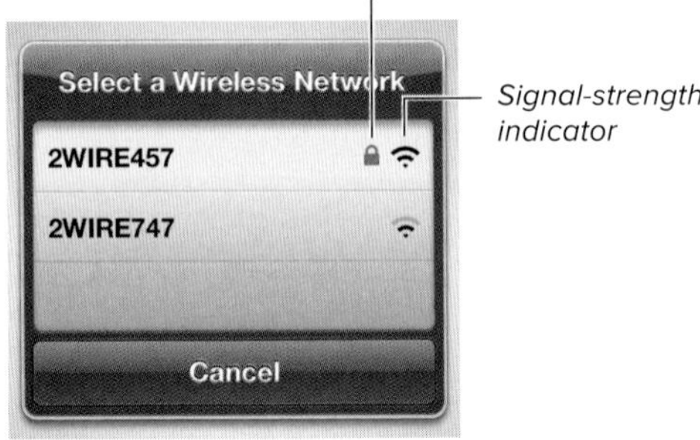

A Available Wi-Fi networks.

Login Screens

Many public-access Wi-Fi hotspots don't require a password but do need you to log in or accept terms of use by using a Web form after you connect. After you join the network, open Safari, and enter any valid Web address. After a few seconds, a login page should appear if you need to sign in (or pay) for access. Many commercial networks in large public places, such as airports and hotels, charge an hourly or daily fee to your credit card.

AirPort Base Stations

If you have an AirPort base station—Apple's brand of wireless router (www.apple.com/wifi)—you can set it up by using the AirPort Setup Assistant. Tap Settings > Wi-Fi, tap the name of your base station (listed below the words *Set up an AirPort base station*), and then follow the onscreen instructions. The base station must be powered on, within range, and as-yet unconfigured.

If your AirPort base station is already set up, you can use the free AirPort Utility app to change its settings and monitor its status: Open App Store, type **airport utility** in the Search field, and then download the app.

These features also work with Time Capsule, Apple's wireless backup drive.

You can also connect to a Wi-Fi network manually (and view or change network settings) by tapping Settings > Wi-Fi. A manual connection is necessary to join a *closed* network—one whose security-minded owner has hidden the network name so that it isn't shown in the list of scanned networks **A**.

Some wireless networks use MAC address filtering to restrict access to preapproved computers, devices, and other hardware. To find your iPad's MAC address, tap Settings > General > About > Wi-Fi Address.

After you join a Wi-Fi network, your iPad automatically reconnects to it whenever the network is in range. If more than one previously used network is in range, your iPad rejoins the one last used. You can make your iPad "forget" specific networks (and their passwords) so that it doesn't join them automatically.

To turn Wi-Fi on or off:

1. Tap Settings > Wi-Fi.
2. Tap the toggle switch to turn Wi-Fi on or off.

TIP If you're not using the Internet, you can turn off Wi-Fi to conserve battery power.

To join a Wi-Fi network manually:

1. Tap Settings > Wi-Fi **B**.
2. Tap the name of a network that you want to join.
3. If the network is secured, type its password and then tap Join.

TIP To troubleshoot a Wi-Fi connection, see http://support.apple.com/kb/TS1398.

To always join new Wi-Fi networks manually:

1. Tap Settings > Wi-Fi.
2. Turn off Ask to Join Networks **B**.

   Turning off this setting suppresses the Select a Wireless Network pop-up box **A**, if it's bugging you.

To forget a network so that your iPad doesn't join it automatically:

1. Tap Settings > Wi-Fi.
2. Tap ⊙ next to the target network.
3. Tap Forget This Network **C**.

TIP To clear all your current network settings (including saved networks, Wi-Fi passwords, and VPN settings), tap Settings > General > Reset > Reset Network Settings.

B The Wi-Fi Networks screen is the gateway to Wi-Fi connections, options, and technical information.

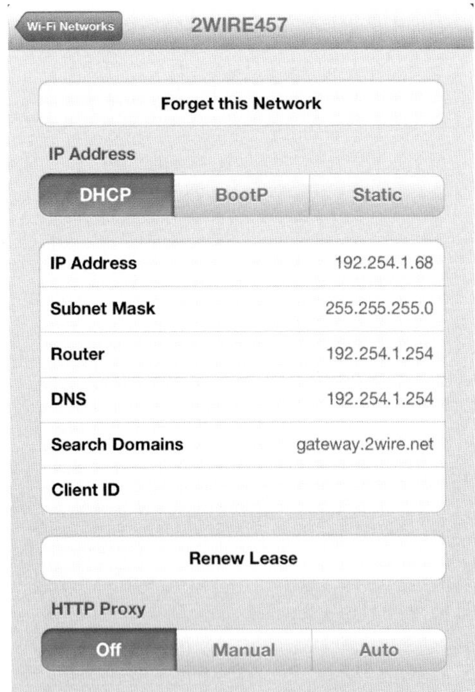

C This screen also lets you adjust advanced network settings. You can set an HTTP proxy, define static network settings, turn on BootP, or renew the settings from a DHCP server.

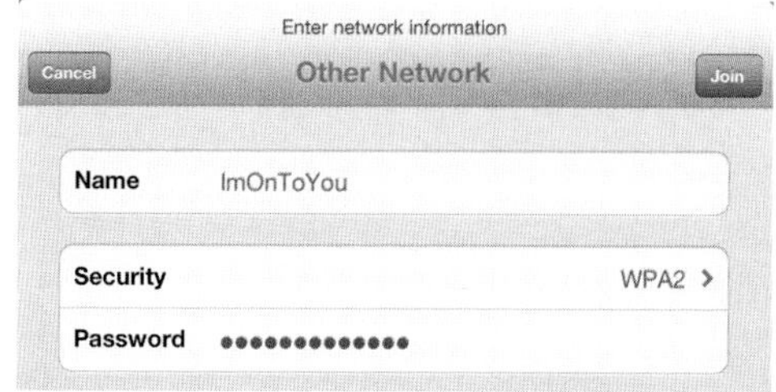

D Before you can join a closed network, the network's owner or administrator must tell you its settings.

To join a closed (hidden) Wi-Fi network:

1. Tap Settings > Wi-Fi > Other.
2. Enter the network name, security (encryption) type, and (if required) password D.
3. Tap Join.

TIP If you don't have a 4G/3G iPad, you can still connect to a cellular network over Wi-Fi by using a *mobile hotspot*. This pocket-size gadget offers always-on broadband connections, can connect multiple devices at the same time (like your iPad, mobile phone, and laptop), and isn't necessarily tied to one carrier. Sadly, mobile hotspots are expensive, both to buy and to use. For examples, see the Novatel MiFi (http://nvtl.com) or Sierra Wireless AirCard (http://www.sierrawireless.com).

Airplane Mode

If an airplane's cabin crew asks you to turn off electronic devices to avoid interfering with the flight instruments, tap Settings > Airplane Mode > On E to suppress your iPad's Wi-Fi, cellular, Bluetooth, and GPS signals. You can still listen to music, watch videos, read books, type notes, and do other non-Internet things.

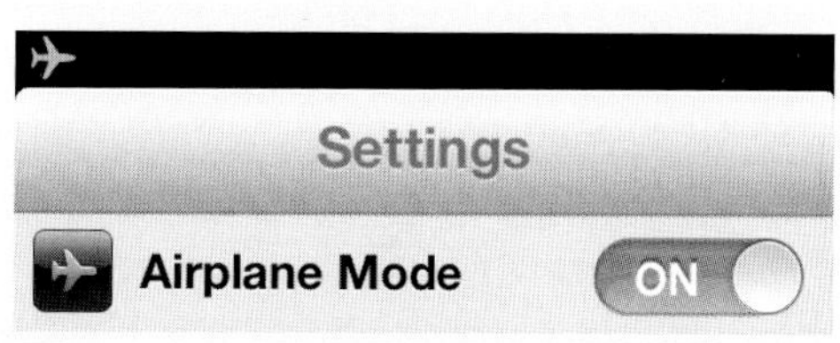

E Activating airplane mode.

If the plane offers in-flight Wi-Fi, tap Settings > Wi-Fi > On. If you're using a Bluetooth accessory, tap Settings > General > Bluetooth > On.

When airplane mode is on, ✈ appears in the status bar at the top of the screen.

When you're not using the Internet, airplane mode is also a quick way to turn off all your iPad's battery-draining wireless services in one shot.

Making Cellular Connections

If you have a 4G/3G iPad, you don't need a Wi-Fi hotspot to connect to the Internet. You can connect wherever your chosen carrier provides cellular network coverage. Before you can start using a cellular network, you must sign up for a prepaid data plan.

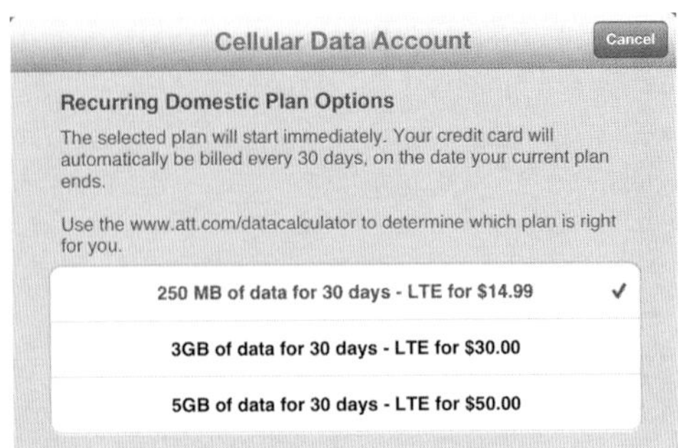

A Sample data plans and fees for AT&T in the United States.

Deciding on a plan

Plans vary by carrier and country, and they change over time. In the United States, for example, the available iPad carriers are AT&T and Verizon; in Canada, they're Bell, Rogers, and Telus. You choose a plan when you set up a new carrier account on your iPad, but you may want to research plans and terms beforehand on the carrier's Web site and search the Web for service reviews by other users.

When you choose a plan, note the following:

- The plan's monthly fee **A**.
- The plan's monthly data limit (250 MB, 2 GB, 3 GB, 5 GB, 10 GB, or whatever). Limits apply to data coming to and going from your iPad. Some carrier Web sites offer a data calculator to help you estimate your data use based on your typical online activities.
- What happens if you exceed the limit. Some plans labeled Unlimited actually impose very large limits rather than being truly unlimited.
- The type of network, and its upload and download speeds.

- Whether you can cancel at any time.
- Whether the plan renews automatically, charging your credit card every month until you remember to cancel manually.
- Whether the plan also provides free, unlimited access to the carrier's public Wi-Fi hotspots, if applicable. AT&T, for example, provides Wi-Fi hotspots in McDonald's restaurants, Starbucks coffee shops, and major airports.
- Whether you can add the plan to your overall bill, if you already have an account with the carrier.

TIP You can't use a cellular data plan to make ordinary phone calls, as you would with an iPhone, but you can make calls with VoIP (voice over IP) apps like Skype.

SIM Cards

A SIM card **B** in some 4G/3G iPad models is used for cellular data. In the United States, for example, cellular service from AT&T requires a SIM card. (Verizon iPads don't use one.)

A SIM (Subscriber Identity Module) card stores information about your cellular account. You can install a card yourself if it wasn't preinstalled or replace it if you change carriers. iPads use the tiny version of a standard SIM card called a micro-SIM card.

Look for the small, looped piece of wire—called a SIM eject tool—stuck to the iPad's documentation folder. Insert the pin into a tiny hole on the left edge of the iPad to pop open the SIM tray. Pull out the SIM tray to install or replace the SIM card. If you don't have a SIM eject tool, use a bent paper clip.

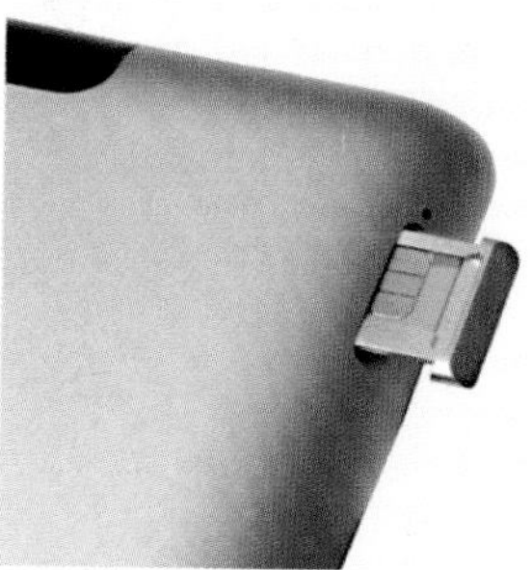

B SIM card.

Signing up for a plan

You can sign up directly from your iPad. The account sign-up process is managed by the carrier, not Apple. Your carrier account is a new account, separate from any of your other wireless, iTunes, or Apple accounts.

To set up a new cellular data account:

1. Tap Settings > Cellular Data **C**.
2. Turn on Cellular Data.

   (If Cellular Data is turned off, all data services use only Wi-Fi.)
3. Tap View Account and then follow the onscreen instructions **D**.

   After you submit your information, your carrier processes it and, if all goes well, activates your data plan. You can access the Internet anywhere you have cellular reception **E**. In an area where both Wi-Fi and cellular work, Wi-Fi prevails. Wi-Fi doesn't count toward the data limit even if cellular service is active.

TIP ***No Service*** **means that you're out of network range (or you've forgotten to activate cellular data by tapping Settings > Cellular Data > On). To troubleshoot a cellular data connection, see http://support.apple.com/kb/TS3780.**

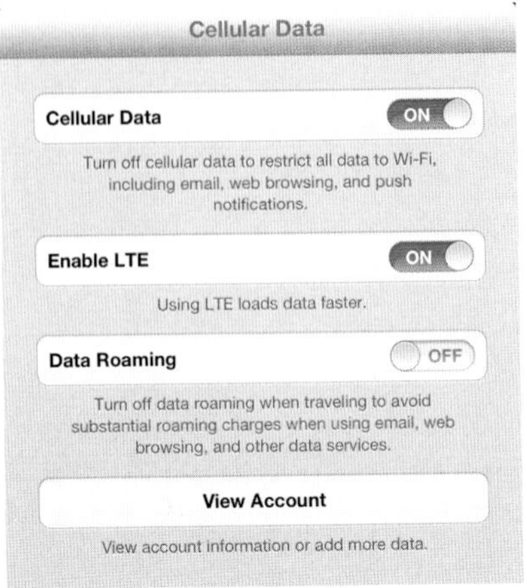

C The Cellular Data screen lets you activate, view, or change your cellular data account and control cellular network access.

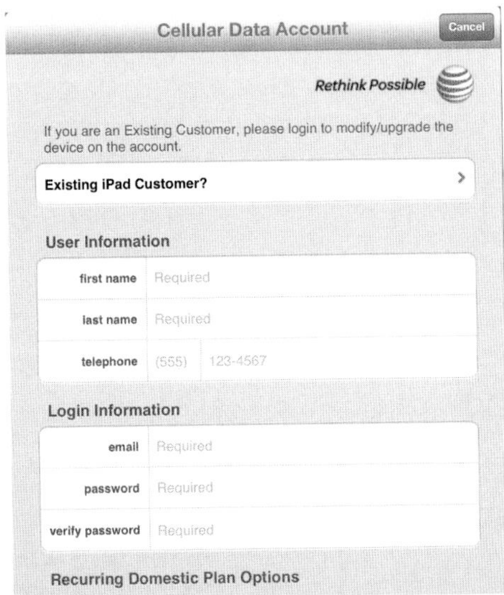

D Scroll to enter user and login information, choose a data plan, enter credit-card and billing information, and agree to terms of service.

E When you're using your cellular network, the status bar at the top of the screen shows the signal strength (more bars = stronger signal) and network/carrier.

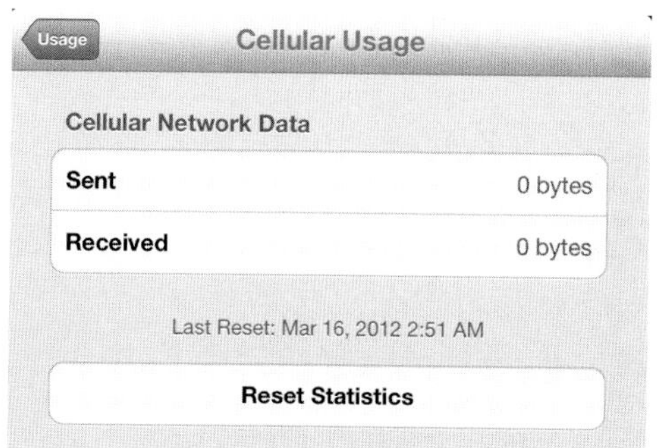

F The Cellular Usage screen shows data downloaded (received) and uploaded (sent). To restart the counts from zero, tap Reset Statistics.

Reducing Data Use

Here are some tips for reducing your data use:

- **Fetch new data manually instead of automatically.** Tap Settings > Mail, Contacts, Calendars > Fetch New Data > Manually.
- **Disable push notifications.** Tap Settings > Notifications, tap an app in the list, and then turn off notifications for that app.
- **Temporarily disable cellular data when you don't need it.** Tap Settings > Cellular Data > Off.
- **Turn off data roaming.** To avoid huge charges for inadvertently roaming onto a third-party cellular network when you travel to other countries, tap Settings > Cellular Data > Data Roaming > Off.

Transferring a data plan

If you need to transfer your cellular data plan to a new iPad, it may be as easy as moving the SIM card from your old iPad to your new one (see the sidebar "SIM Cards" earlier in this chapter). If your plan doesn't use a SIM card, contact your carrier, and explain that you need to transfer service to a new iPad. After the carrier transfers your service, on the new iPad, tap Settings > General > Reset > Reset Subscriber Service > Reprovision Account. Restart your iPad if the plan doesn't autoactivate within 2 minutes.

Some carriers let you lock down the SIM card by adding a PIN code to it so that others can't use it. Tap Settings > Cellular Data > SIM PIN (if it appears) and then pick a number. If the SIM already has a PIN, contact your carrier.

Monitoring data use

If you're on a limited monthly data plan, the iPad displays pop-up warnings as you approach the limit. You can also view your data use at any time and see how many days are left in the billing period.

To view your cellular data use:

- Tap Settings > Cellular Data > Usage **F**.

Changing or canceling data plans

You can upgrade or downgrade to another plan, add a block of extra gigabytes to your existing plan, cancel your plan, or change your credit-card number. If you plan to travel, some carriers offer international plans.

To change or cancel your data plan:

1. Tap Settings > Cellular Data > View Account.
2. Sign in with the same email address and password that you used when you originally set up the account.
3. Tap Add Data or Change Plan.

Using Personal Hotspot

On 4G models of iPad 3 or later, you can use the Personal Hotspot feature to share your iPad's Internet connection with other people and devices at the same time—mobile phones, laptops, iPhones, iPods, or other Internet-enabled devices. Personal Hotspot can also share an Internet connection with a computer connected to your iPad via Bluetooth or USB (a practice also known as *tethering*). For service details, contact your carrier, and expect to pay extra.

To share an Internet connection, make sure that you're connected to a cellular network and then tap Settings > General > Network > Set Up Personal Hotspot (if it appears). After you set up your account, tap Settings > Personal Hotspot > On. You can set a password (at least eight characters) and decide how other devices (up to five) connect to your hotspot:

- **Wi-Fi.** On the device or computer, choose your iPad from the list of available Wi-Fi networks.
- **Bluetooth.** On your iPad, tap Settings > General > Bluetooth > On. Follow the instructions that came with the device to pair it with your iPad.
- **USB.** Connect the computer to your iPad by using the dock connector–to–USB cable. In the computer's Network preferences or control panel, choose your iPad and then configure the network settings.

The name of your hotspot is the name of your iPad (tap Settings > General > About > Name). When Personal Hotspot is on, appears in the status bar at the top of the screen. When a device is connected, a blue bar appears on the hotspot screen, listing the number of connected devices.

An active personal hotspot drains your battery fast and can easily blow through your data plan's use limit. To check use, tap Settings > Cellular Data > Usage.

TIP To troubleshoot Personal Hotspot, see http://support.apple.com/kb/TS2756.

Using Virtual Private Networks

A *virtual private network* (VPN) lets you connect from your iPad to an organization's network securely and privately by using the Internet as a conduit. VPN works over both Wi-Fi and cellular data network connections.

To add a new VPN configuration:

1. Tap Settings > General > Network > VPN.
2. Turn on VPN.
3. Tap Add VPN Configuration.
4. Configure the VPN connection based on information you get from your network administrator or your organization's IT department Ⓐ.

TIP You can add multiple VPN configurations and switch among them on the VPN screen. When a VPN connection is active, VPN appears in the status bar at the top of the screen. When you're not using VPN, turn it off to conserve power (tap Settings > General > Network > VPN > Off).

Ⓐ If you've set up a VPN on your computer, you may be able to use the same VPN settings for your iPad.

Using Bluetooth Devices

Bluetooth is a wireless technology that provides short-range (up to 33 feet) radio links between an iPad and external keyboards, headphones, speakers, or other Bluetooth-equipped devices. It eliminates cable clutter while simplifying communications, sharing, and data synchronization between devices. Bluetooth doesn't need a line-of-sight connection, so you can, say, use a hands-free headset to listen to music playing on the iPad in your backpack.

A *passkey* (or personal identification number [PIN]) is a number that associates your iPad with a Bluetooth device. For security, many Bluetooth devices make you use a passkey to ensure that your iPad is connecting to your device and not someone else's nearby. Check the device's manual for a passkey.

Before you can use a Bluetooth device, you must make it discoverable and then pair it with your iPad; the device will come with instructions. *Pairing* (or *passkey exchange*) gets the iPad to positively identify the device that you want to connect to. After it's paired, the device autoconnects whenever it's within range of your iPad.

You can pair your iPad with multiple devices at the same time—say, a headset and a keyboard—if all the devices are different types. (You can't pair two keyboards simultaneously, for example.) If you want to use a different device of the same type, you must unpair the first device.

TIP **To connect a Bluetooth keyboard, see "Using a Wireless Keyboard" in Chapter 2.**

To pair a Bluetooth device with an iPad:

1. Follow the instructions that came with the device to make it discoverable.
2. Tap Settings > General > Bluetooth > On.

   When you turn on Bluetooth, the iPad finds nearby discoverable devices and displays them in the Devices list.
3. Tap the device in the Devices list and then type the requested passkey to complete the pairing **A**.

   Check the device's manual for the passkey.

TIP Some Bluetooth audio devices come with a small separate transceiver that plugs into the iPad's headphone jack. If you have one of these transceivers, you don't need to turn on Bluetooth; the plug-in takes care of the connection.

To unpair a device from an iPad:

1. Tap Settings > General > Bluetooth,
2. Tap ⊙ next to the device name.
3. Tap Forget This Device.

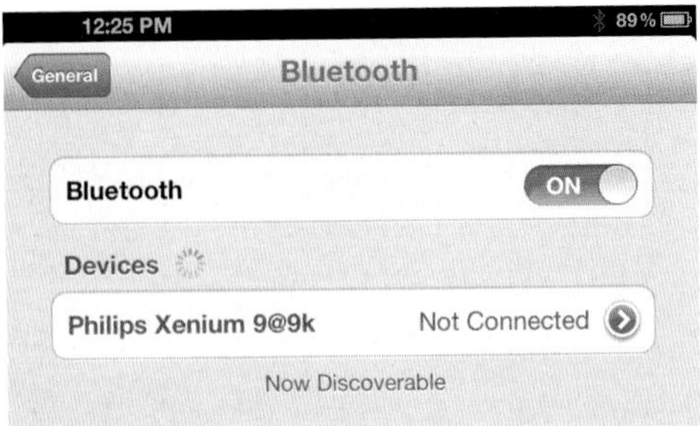

A To confirm the pairing, the iPad displays the device's name in the Bluetooth screen.

Bluetooth Status

When a Bluetooth device is connected, the Bluetooth icon ✱ appears in the status bar at the top of the screen. The icon's color reflects its status. A white icon means that Bluetooth is on and paired with a device. A gray icon means that Bluetooth is on and paired with a device, but the device is out of range or turned off.

When you're not using Bluetooth, turn it off to conserve power. To do so, tap Settings > General > Bluetooth > Off.

(A) AirPlay wirelessly streams files to AirPlay-compatible audio and video devices like Apple TV.

Streaming with AirPlay

The iPad can stream music, photos, videos, or compatible apps to external speakers or displays via *AirPlay,* Apple's wireless file-streaming technology. You can stream to any AirPlay-compatible device on the same Wi-Fi network as your iPad. You can also use AirPlay to stream audio to an Apple AirPort base station (wireless router).

To stream content to an AirPlay-equipped device:

1. Start the music, slideshow, or video.
2. Tap on the iPad's screen.
3. Choose the AirPlay device (such as Apple TV).

   After streaming starts on the device (A), you can switch away from the iPad app that's playing the content.

To use the AirPlay playback controls:

1. Double-click the Home button to show the multitasking bar at the bottom of the screen.
2. Flick left to right to access the playback controls (play, pause, volume, and so on).

To switch playback to the iPad:

1. Tap .
2. Choose iPad.

   All audio and video output return to the iPad.

Screen Mirroring

The iPad 2 or later can *mirror* (duplicate) whatever is on its screen—videos, apps, games, photos, presentations, Web sites, anything—to a high-definition TV (HDTV), digital projector, or other display. All you need is an Apple Digital AV Adapter **A**. Plug it in to your iPad and then connect it to an HDMI cable from the TV or display; mirroring is enabled automatically **B**. (Don't forget to change the TV's input source to HDMI.) If you own an Apple TV, you can mirror the iPad screen over Wi-Fi.

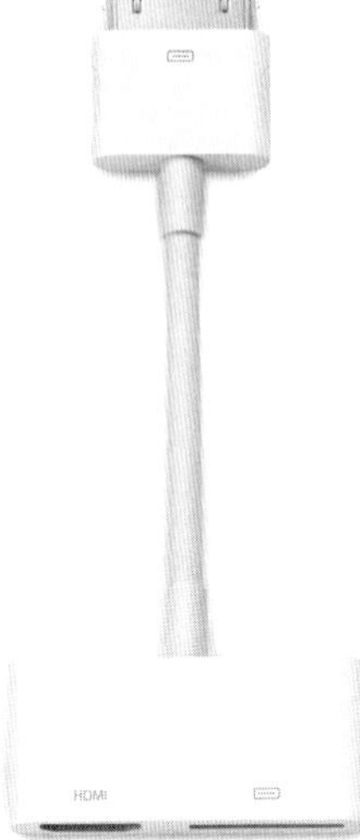

A The Apple Digital AV Adapter is a simple, portable tool that mirrors what's on your iPad screen to an HDTV or HDMI-compatible display. (For an older VGA display, use the Apple VGA Adapter.)

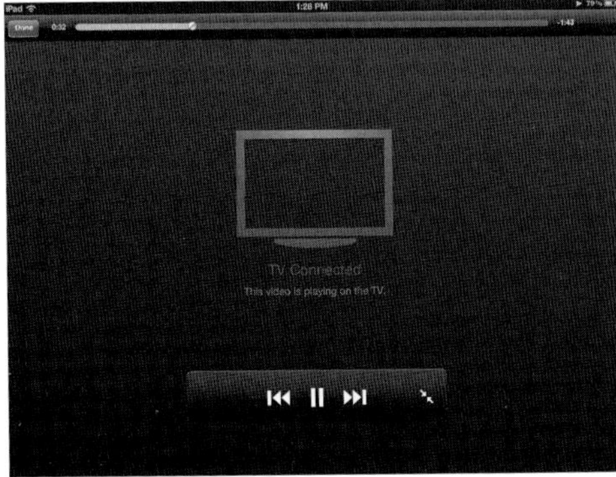

B You can control playback by using the controls on the iPad's screen.

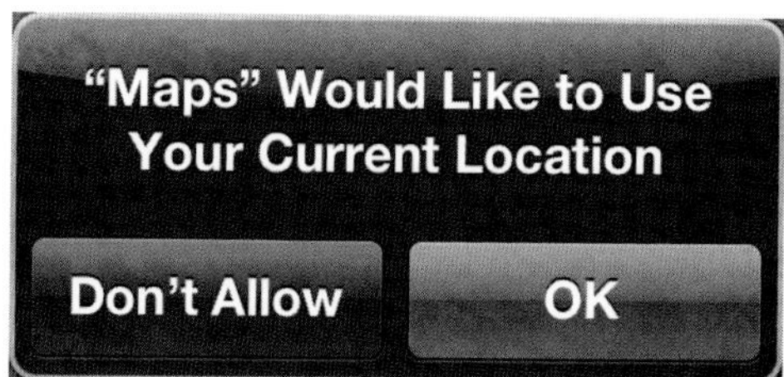

A No matter which option you choose here, you can change it in the Locations Services screen.

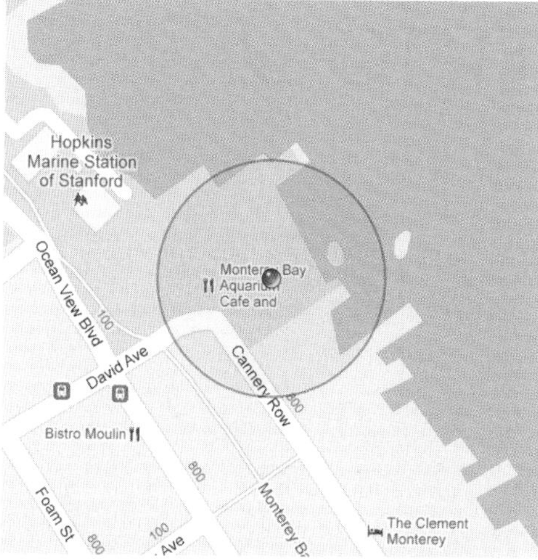

B The circle around your current location indicates how accurately Location Services can determine your position. The circle can grow or shrink over time or as you walk or drive around.

Using Location Services

Location Services lets apps use your physical whereabouts via the iPad's built-in positioning service. Built-in apps such as Reminders, Maps, Safari, and Camera use Location Services, as do many third-party apps—particularly weather, travel, search, movie-time, real-estate, and social-networking apps.

Location Services determines your approximate location by using the iPad's built-in digital compass and data from nearby Wi-Fi hotspots. On 4G/3G models, it also uses Assisted GPS (Global Positioning System satellites) and data from cellular networks (cell towers).

The first time an app makes a request to use Location Services, your iPad pops open a location warning for that app **A**. To let the app locate you, tap OK; otherwise, tap Don't Allow. Your response sticks, and the request isn't shown again (unless you later reset all location warnings by tapping Settings > General > Reset > Reset Location Warnings).

Location Services does its best to locate you by combining compass, Wi-Fi, cellular, and GPS data. Depending on data quality and other factors (such as interference from your surroundings), your location may be unavailable or inaccurate. Apps that show your location onscreen, including Maps, indicate your current approximate location with a blue dot. A blue circle around the dot, if present, indicates how precisely your location can be determined. The smaller the circle, the greater the precision **B**.

continues on next page

If you don't want to be found, or if you want to conserve battery power, you can turn off Location Services or disable it for specific apps. To do so, tap Settings > Location Services and then tap the appropriate toggle switch or switches **C**. An app won't appear in the Location Services list until it makes its first location request **A**.

When an app is using Location Services, ➤ appears in the status bar at the top of the screen. To hide this icon (or to set other options), tap Settings > Location Services > System Services.

Location Services
Location Services
ON
Location Services uses crowd-sourced Wi-Fi hotspot locations to determine your approximate location.
Camera
ON
Craigslist
OFF
Google Earth
OFF
Maps
ON
RadarUS
ON
Safari
OFF
Tide Graph HD
ON
Trailers
ON
Yelp
ON
Zillow
OFF
Find My iPad
Off
A purple location services icon will appear next to an item that is currently using your location.
A gray location services icon will appear next to an item that has used your location within the last 24 hours.
An outlined location services icon will appear next to an item that is using a geofence.
A geofence is a virtual perimeter around a location. Apps like Reminders use geofencing to notify you when you arrive at, or leave, these locations.
System Services

C You can turn Location Services off for some or for all apps and services. If you turn off Location Services, you're prompted to turn it on again the next time an app or service tries to use it.

Surveillance

Apple collects location data but says that it doesn't identify you personally. Third-party apps are a different story. Each one has its own privacy policy which, like Apple's privacy policy, can change with the wind. Note also that your iPad's location information can be collected and used regardless of whether you enable Location Services—ostensibly for safety purposes, to locate you in an emergency to aid response efforts.

If you use Location Services, assume that you can always be tracked and that your location data could be sold to third parties or given to police or governments.

Managing Your Data

You can use your iPad's data-management apps and services to:

- Use iCloud to sync your important data—contacts, Internet bookmarks, reminders, notes, and more—across your devices.
- Sync with iTunes to copy content from your iPad to your Mac or Windows PC, and vice versa.
- Back up your data with iCloud or iTunes, and restore it if necessary.
- Copy files between your iPad and computer.
- Update your iPad's operating system (iOS) when Apple releases a new version.
- Get technical, storage, data-use, and other information about your iPad.
- Get push notifications from apps that are trying to get your attention.

In This Chapter

Using iCloud

iCloud is an online storage and computing service that uploads (copies) your content to Apple's remote data center and pushes it wirelessly to your Mac, Windows PC, and iOS devices (iPad, iPhone, and iPod touch) **A**. Your music, photos, documents, and more are available on demand across all your computers and iDevices. iCloud is integrated with your apps and works in the background silently and automatically, without manual syncing or sending. You can also view and manage your content and settings by visiting https://www.icloud.com in a modern browser. Some iCloud features work across OS X, Windows, and iOS, whereas others are iOS-only.

iCloud identifies you by your Apple ID and provides unlimited free storage for purchased music, TV shows, iOS apps, and books. It also includes 5 GB of free storage for mail, documents, and backups. Higher storage capacities are available for an annual fee. You can manage your storage by controlling backups and choosing which documents to store in the cloud.

TIP iCloud secures your content by encrypting it. For details, see http://support.apple.com/kb/HT4865.

To set up iCloud:

1. Tap Settings > iCloud.
2. Sign in with your Apple ID and password.
3. Turn on the services that you want to enable **B**.

A Apple's graphical depiction of iCloud. Changes made on one device are pushed to the cloud (a remote data center) and then synced automatically with your other devices.

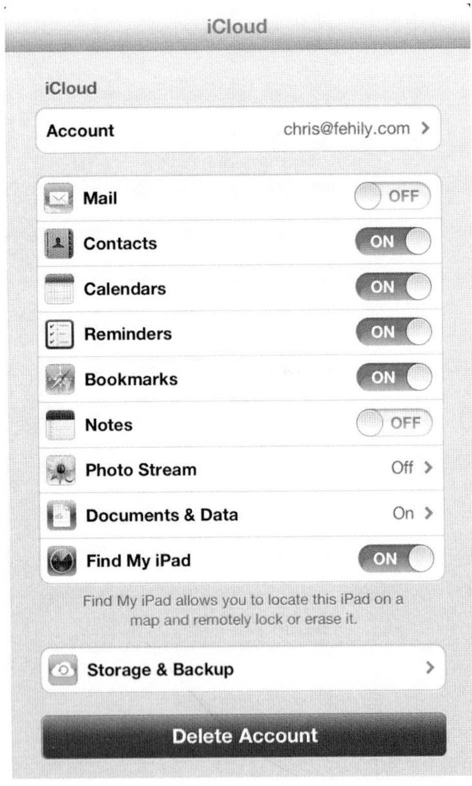

B iCloud settings include On/Off switches for the types of data that can be synced. Tapping Photo Stream or Documents & Data brings up additional options for those features.

Using iCloud services

The following iCloud services are available:

- **Mail, Contacts, Calendars, Reminders, and Notes.** Sync data from these apps to your other devices.
- **Bookmarks.** Sync your Safari bookmarks and Reading List to your other devices.
- **Photo Stream.** Photos that you take on one device appear automatically on all your devices that have Photo Stream enabled. Photo Stream keeps 1,000 photos, including the last 30 days' worth of new photos. To view your photos, delete them, share them, or move them to Camera Roll or to an album (before they're rotated out by new photos), open the Photos app, tap Photo Stream at the top of the screen, and then tap .
- **Documents & Data.** Sync Apple iWork (Pages, Keynote, and Numbers) documents for transfer between your computer and iOS devices. Open a Web browser, go to https://www.icloud.com, sign in to iCloud, and then click the iWork icon on the main page. All your iWork for iOS documents will be there, complete with your most recent edits. Turn on iCloud separately for each iWork app. If Pages is installed on your iPad, for example, tap Settings > Pages > Use iCloud > On. Third-party developers can make their apps work with Documents & Data too.

continues on next page

- **Find My iPad.** Locate a missing iPad. For details, see "Securing Your iPad" in Chapter 1.
- **Storage & Backup.** To make an iCloud backup, tap Storage & Backup and then turn on iCloud Backup **C**. iCloud automatically backs up important data on your iPad daily over Wi-Fi when your iPad is connected to a power source and is screen-locked. To back up manually, tap Back Up Now.

TIP If you're using iCloud on a Mac or Windows PC, you must set it up separately on your computer. On OS X, choose Apple menu > System Preferences > iCloud. On Windows, download and install the iCloud Control Panel from http://support.apple.com/kb/DL1455, and then choose Control Panel > Network and Internet > iCloud.

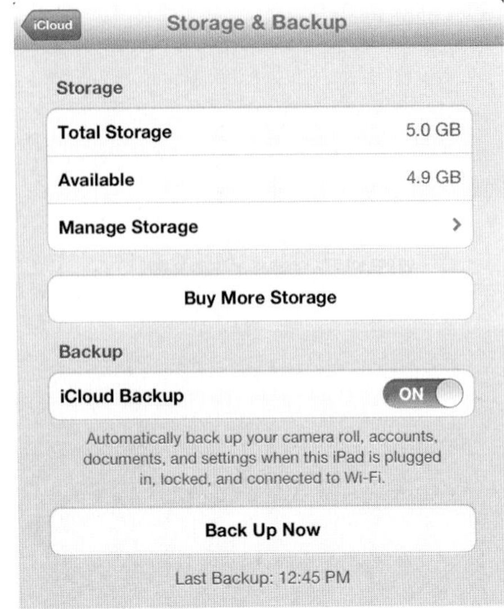

C To select which apps back up their data and see how much storage space each application is using, tap Manage Storage. If you need more iCloud storage, tap Buy More Storage.

iCloud Backups

When you turn on Storage & Backup, iCloud backs up the following items:

- Purchased music, TV shows, apps, and books (to which the 5 GB storage limit doesn't apply)
- Photos and video in the Camera Roll
- Device settings (such as those for Mail, Contacts, Calendars accounts)
- App data
- Home-screen and app organization
- Messages (iMessage, SMS, and MMS)
- Ringtones

When you set up a new iPad, Setup Assistant lets you restore from one of your recent iCloud backups (see "Setting Up Your iPad" in Chapter 1). You can also restore an iCloud backup when you erase your iPad. To do so, tap Settings > General > Reset > Erase All Content and Settings.

The following items are *not* backed up to iCloud but can be synced via using iTunes on a computer (see "Downloading your purchases" later in this chapter):

- Music and TV shows not purchased from the iTunes Store
- Movies, podcasts, and audiobooks
- Photos that were synced from your computer originally

D The Purchased screen lists all the items that you previously purchased from one of the Apple stores. You don't have to pay again for items that you delete and then download again or that you download on multiple devices.

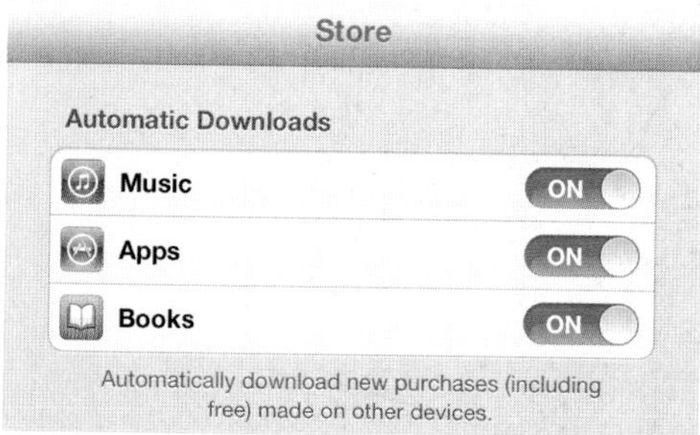

E When these settings are turned on, if you buy an item on, say, your iPhone or iPod touch, that item appears automatically on your iPad (and vice versa).

Downloading your purchases

When iCloud is enabled, you don't have to do much. Changes to contacts, calendars, and reminders, for example, are updated automatically across your devices. Music, TV shows, apps, and books purchased on a different device, however, can be downloaded manually or automatically to your iPad.

To download purchased items manually:

1. On your iPad, open iTunes (for music and TV shows) or App Store (for apps), or tap iBooks > Store (for books).
2. Tap the Purchased button at the bottom of the screen.
3. Tap the iCloud Download button next to the item that you want to download **D**.

To download purchased items automatically:

1. Tap Settings > Store.
2. Turn on Automatic Downloads for music, apps, or books **E**.

Syncing with iTunes

Syncing with iTunes copies content from your iPad to your Mac or Windows PC, and vice versa. You can do all of the following:

- Sync by connecting your iPad to your computer, using the dock connector–to–USB cable that came with your iPad.
- Set up iTunes to sync wirelessly over Wi-Fi.
- Sync music, photos, video, podcasts, apps, and more.
- Change your sync options at any time.

Each time you sync, content is synced between your iPad and computer to reflect new, updated, or deleted content.

Before you sync, update to the latest versions of iOS on your iPad (tap Settings > General > Software Update) and iTunes on your computer (visit www.apple.com/itunes/download).

To sync with iTunes via USB cable:

1. Connect your iPad to your computer via USB cable.
2. Open iTunes on your computer.
3. In the iTunes sidebar (on the left side), click your iPad in the Devices list **A**.
4. In the main section of the iTunes window, click the content tabs **B** (Info, Apps, Music, Movies, and so on), and configure sync options for each one.

TIP Don't sync items (such as contacts, calendars, and notes) that you're already syncing with iCloud. If you do, those items may be duplicated on your iPad.

A It may take a moment for your iPad to appear in the iTunes sidebar.

B Some tabs may not appear if you don't have corresponding content in your iTunes library.

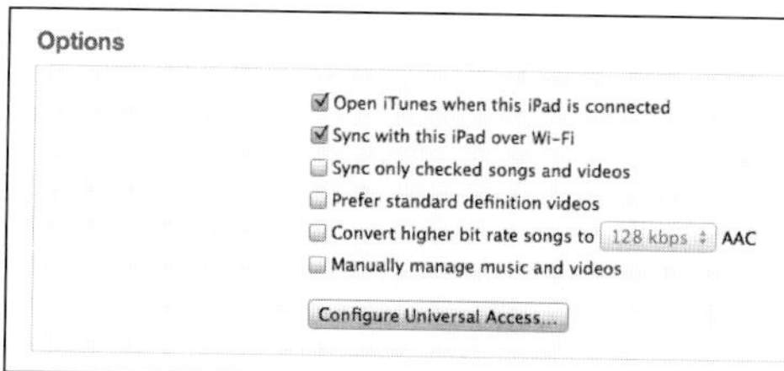

C When wireless sync is enabled, your iPad will appear in the iTunes sidebar whenever your computer and iPad are on the same Wi-Fi network.

5. To sync, click Apply or Sync in the bottom-right corner of the iTunes window.

   Don't disconnect your iPad from the computer while the iPad screen says *Sync in Progress*. You can cancel the current sync by dragging the Cancel Sync slider on the iPad's screen.

To sync with iTunes via Wi-Fi:

1. Connect your iPad to your computer.
2. Open iTunes on your computer.
3. In the iTunes sidebar (on the left side), click your iPad in the Devices list A.
4. In the main section of the iTunes window, click the Summary tab and then select Sync with This iPad over Wi-Fi C.
5. To sync manually, tap Settings > General > iTunes Wi-Fi Sync > Sync Now.

   Your iPad will also sync automatically at least once a day when your iPad is plugged in to power, iTunes is open on your computer, or your iPad and the computer are on the same Wi-Fi network.
6. When your iPad appears in the iTunes sidebar, click the content tabs B (Apps, Music, Movies, TV Shows, and so on), and configure sync options.
7. To sync, click Apply or Sync in the bottom-right corner of the iTunes window.

   Don't disconnect your iPad from the computer while the iPad screen says *Sync in Progress*. You can cancel the current sync by dragging the Cancel Sync slider on the iPad's screen.

TIP To troubleshoot Wi-Fi syncing, see http://support.apple.com/kb/TS4062.

Backing up in iTunes

iTunes create backups of your iPad when you

- Sync with iTunes (disabled if you have iCloud backup turned on).
- Right-click your iPad in the iTunes sidebar (on the left) and then choose Back Up.

To restore a backup, connect your iPad to your computer via USB cable, right-click your iPad in the iTunes sidebar, and then choose Restore from Backup.

When you set up a new iPad, Setup Assistant lets you restore from one of your recent iTunes backups (see "Setting Up Your iPad" in Chapter 1). You can also restore an iTunes backup when you erase your iPad. To do so, tap Settings > General > Reset > Erase All Content and Settings.

To transfer a backup from your current iPad to a new iPad, see http://support.apple.com/kb/HT2109. This article applies to iPads as well as iPhones.

Managing content manually

By default, iTunes automatically syncs your entire iTunes library whenever you connect your iPad to your computer. You can also manage songs and videos on your iPad manually, choosing just the items that you want to have with you (handy if your entire iTunes library is too big to fit on your iPad).

To add an item to your iPad, drag it from your iTunes library to the iPad icon in the Devices list of the iTunes sidebar Ⓐ.

To configure your iPad to manage content manually:

1. Connect your iPad to your computer via USB cable.
2. Open iTunes on your computer.
3. In the Devices list of the iTunes sidebar, click your iPad (A).
4. In the main section of the iTunes window, click the Summary tab and then select Manually Manage Music and Videos (C).
5. Click Apply or Sync in the bottom-right corner of the iTunes window.

TIP When you connect your iPad, you can temporarily override the manual setting: Press Command+Option (Mac) or Shift+Ctrl (Windows) until your iPad appears in the iTunes sidebar.

TIP Even when manual management is turned on, you can still sync some content automatically. Select any content tab, such as Video, to enable automatic syncing for that type of content.

Copying Files Between Your iPad and Your Computer

The File Sharing feature lets you copy files between your iPad and computer, using iTunes as a conduit. You can share files created with a compatible app and saved in a supported format. Not all apps support this feature; see each app's documentation to find out how it shares files.

In iTunes on your computer, apps that support file sharing appear in the File Sharing section at the bottom of the Apps tab. For each app in the apps, the Files list shows the documents that are on your iPad.

To copy files between your iPad and your computer:

1. Connect your iPad to your computer via USB cable.
2. Open iTunes on your computer.
3. In the Devices list of the iTunes sidebar (on the left side), click your iPad.

   It may take a moment for your iPad to appear in the sidebar.
4. In the main section of the iTunes window, click the Apps tab.

5. In the File Sharing section, click an app in the Apps list on the left **A**.

   The files for the selected app appear in the documents list on the right.

6. Do any of the following:

   - Copy a file from your iPad to your computer: Select it in the Files list and then click Save To.
   - Drag files from the Files list to the computer's desktop or to a folder window (or vice versa).
   - Delete a file from your iPad: Select it in the Files list and then press your computer's Delete key.
   - Copy a file from your computer to your iPad: Click Add.

TIP To select multiple files in the Files list, hold down the Ctrl key (Windows) or the Command key (Mac) and then click the desired files. Click again to deselect a file. To select a range of adjacent files, hold down the Shift key, click the first file in the range, and then click the last file.

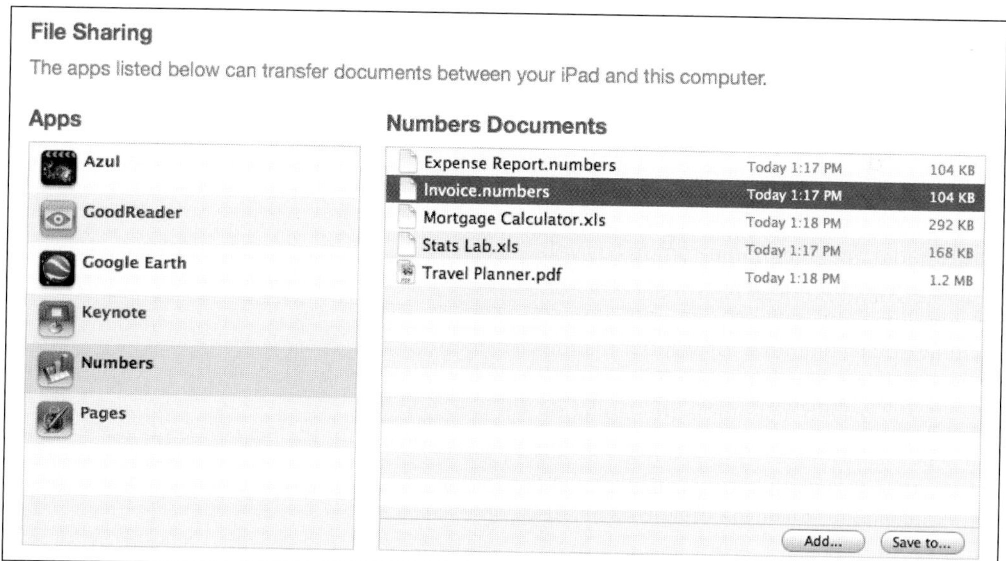

A File Sharing lets you copy files between your iPad and computer, and delete files from your iPad.

Updating iOS

iOS is Apple's mobile operating system, which runs on iPads, iPhones, iPod touches, and Apple TV. Apple regularly releases free updates and bug fixes for iOS. Some changes add features to iOS and the built-in apps, whereas others plug security holes or fix stability problems. You can update to the latest version of iOS over Wi-Fi.

To see your iOS version:

- Tap Settings > General > About.

  The version number and the build number (in parentheses) are listed next to the Version label.

To update iOS:

1. Connect your iPad to a power source or fully charge the battery.
2. Connect to a Wi-Fi network by tapping Settings > Wi-Fi.

   For details, see "Making Wi-Fi Connections" in Chapter 3.
3. Tap Settings > General > Software Update.
4. If a newer version of iOS is available, follow the onscreen instructions to download and install the update.

TIP If your iPad is connected to your computer, you can update iOS from the Summary tab of iTunes on your computer.

A If you're running low on space, use the Usage screen to finger the storage hogs.

Getting Information About Your iPad

The Settings app provides technical, storage, data-use, and other diagnostic information about your iPad.

To get general information:

- Tap Settings > General > About to get information about your iPad, including available storage space, serial numbers, and network addresses.

  You can also view or turn off diagnostic information that's sent to Apple.

To see or change the name of your iPad:

- Tap Settings > General > About > Name.

  The name appears in the iTunes sidebar when your iPad is connected to iTunes and it's being used by iCloud, Personal Hotspot, or other services.

To view storage, battery charge, and data use:

- Tap Settings > General > Usage to view available storage space, the percentage of battery power remaining, and (on 4G/3G models) cellular data use **A**.

TIP **If your iPad is connected to your computer, you can also view information on the Summary tab of iTunes on your computer.**

Getting Notifications

Certain apps can push notifications to you, even when you're not actively using the app. Notification Center is the central list of all the apps that are trying to get your attention. Apps that can send notifications include

- Calendar (for events and invitations)
- Reminders (for reminders coming due)
- Game Center (for friend requests and game invitations)
- Mail (for incoming email)
- Messages (for new messages)
- FaceTime (for missed calls)
- Twitter (for direct messages and mentions)
- Any third-party apps whose developers tap into Notification Center

Notifications come in two forms: banners and alerts. A banner slides into view from the top of the screen and then disappears after 5 seconds **A**. An alert pops open center-screen and stays there until you acknowledge it by tapping Close, View, Snooze, or whatever. Tapping a banner opens the corresponding app to show the related item. (If you tap a Mail subject heading, for example, Mail opens and displays that message.) If a notification appears in the Lock screen, flick it from left to right to respond to it.

If a banner notification disappears before you can get to it, you can open Notification Center at any time to see a list of recent notifications.

To show Notification Center:

- Flick down from the top of the screen **B**.

To remove a notification:

1. Tap ⊗.
2. Tap Clear.

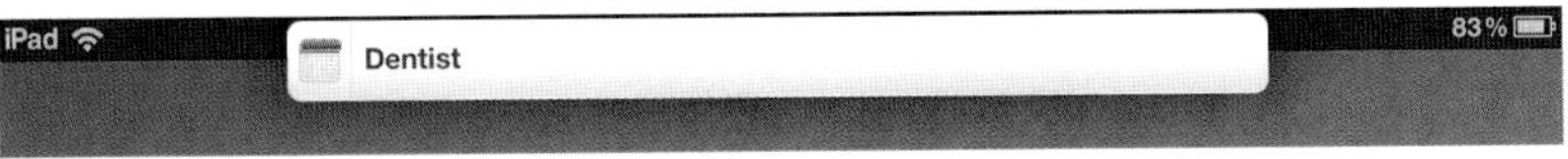

A A banner notification disappears by itself after a few seconds.

B Notification Center lists recent notifications. Flick up the screen or tap off Notification Center to dismiss it, or tap a notification to jump to the corresponding app.

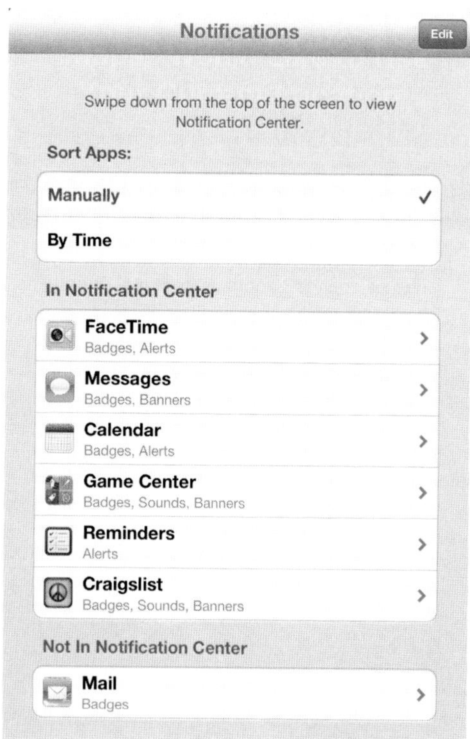

C You can fine-tune how each app displays notifications. Some settings vary by app.

To configure Notification Center:

1. Tap Settings > Notifications.

   Apps that can send notifications are listed **C**.

2. Tap an app to change any of the following settings:

   - Whether an app sends notifications
   - Whether you receive banner or alert notifications (or none at all)
   - The order in which notifications are listed (tap the Edit button and then drag ≡ up or down to reorder the list)
   - How many recent notifications appear in Notification Center
   - Whether to display a badge (a number in a little red circle) on the notifying app's dock icon
   - Whether the notification appears when your iPad is locked
   - Whether to play a sound as part of the notification

5

App Store

App Store is where you can search for, browse, review, and download programs that run on your iPad. More than half a million free or paid apps from Apple and third-party developers are available, with new or updated apps arriving every day.

The store is curated, meaning that Apple must approve every app. Apple can also yank an app from the store if it crashes too much, violates store policy, is complained about excessively, or whatever. Yanked apps disappear from the store but not from your iPad; after you download an app and back it up, it's yours.

To use App Store, you must be connected to the Internet (Wi-Fi or cellular signal) and have an Apple ID. If you didn't set up an Apple ID when you set up your iPad, tap Settings > Store to sign in to your account or to change or create an Apple ID.

In This Chapter

Finding Apps

You can find apps by using the store's browse and search tools. Apps are available in many languages, though store content varies by country.

TIP Some apps (particularly games) have parental ratings. To prevent children from installing or opening certain apps, tap Settings > General > Restrictions.

To browse for apps:

- In App Store, tap one of the following buttons in the bottom toolbar:

  Featured. The Featured screen shows new and notable apps spotlighted by Apple's staff (via editorial fiat or paid placement). Flick to the bottom of the screen to see staff favorites. Buttons at the top of the screen let you show Apple-featured apps; list popular new apps; or sort apps by name, release date, or popularity **A**.

  Genius. The Genius screen recommends new apps based on the apps you've already downloaded.

  Top Charts. The Top Charts screen lists the currently most popular paid, free, and top-grossing apps in the store **B**. To show more apps, flick left or right in the lists. To show only a certain type of top apps, tap Categories at the top of the screen. These lists are updated many times each day.

TIP The Top Charts and Featured screens usually are the best starting points for browsing for apps.

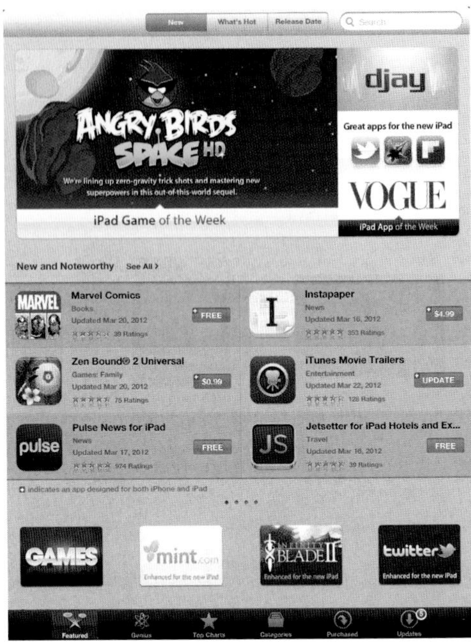

A The Featured screen.

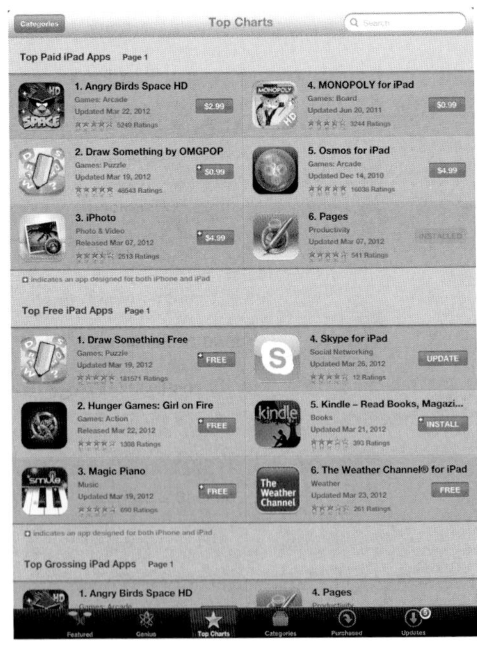

B The Top Charts screen.

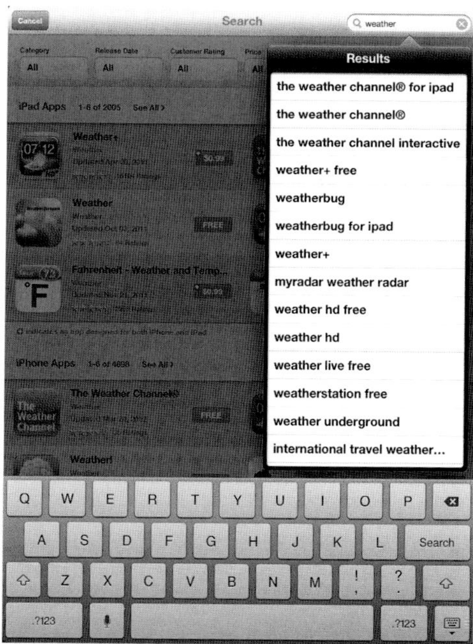

C As you type, the Results list opens to help you complete your search.

Narrowing Search Results

If too many apps are listed, you can do the following:

- Narrow the Results list by tapping the filter buttons near the top of the screen (Category, Release Date, and so on).
- Sort the Results list by tapping the Sort By button.
- Redo your search by adding or refining keywords in the Search field.

Categories. The Categories screen lists apps by type (Games, Productivity, Weather, and so on). Tap a category to see new, popular, featured, or sorted apps in that category.

Purchased. The Purchased screen lists the apps (paid or free) that you've downloaded previously. To restore an app that you deleted, find it in the list and then tap the iCloud icon. You don't have to pay again for previously purchased apps. To hide an app in this screen, flick it left or right.

Updates. The Updates screen list apps that have been updated by their developers since you downloaded them. Updates are free.

TIP Buttons at the bottom of most App Store screens let you log in or out of your Apple ID account, redeem iTunes gift cards, or get technical support for a problem.

To search for apps:

1. In App Store, tap the Search field in the top-right corner of the screen, type one or more keywords, and then tap Search on the keyboard (or tap one of the suggested apps in the drop-down Results list) **C**.

TIP To cancel a search, tap Cancel in the top-left corner of the screen. To clear the Search field, tap ⊗ in that field.

2. Flick left or right to review the Results list.

Downloading Apps

After you find an app, you can download it to your iPad. To avoid carrier charges on 4G/3G models, download or update apps over a Wi-Fi network rather than a cellular network. The number of apps that you can download is limited only by the amount of space available on your iPad.

TIP To sync your app purchases across all your iDevices automatically (if you own more than one device), tap Settings > Store > Apps > On (below Automatic Downloads). For details, see "Using iCloud" in Chapter 4.

To download and install an app:

1. In App Store, browse to or search for the app that you want.
2. (Optional) Tap the app's icon to see its Info screen, where you can read a description, see screen shots, read customer ratings and reviews, send the app to someone as a gift, and more **A**.

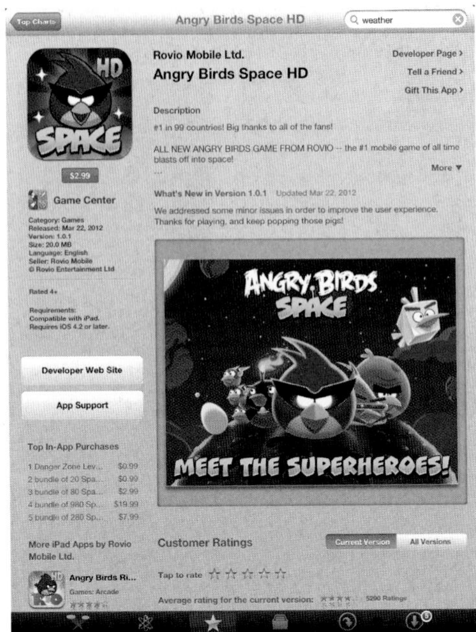

A You can read an app's Info screen before you buy.

Getting Apps from iTunes

You can also download apps in iTunes on your computer. When the download completes, the app appears in the Apps section of your iTunes library (listed in the sidebar) and is installed on your iPad the next time you sync, provided that your computer is authorized with the same Apple ID that you used to download the apps from the store. Similarly, any apps that you download directly on your iPad are added to your iTunes library automatically the next time you sync. Apps that you delete from your iPad or iTunes library are synced too.

For details, see "Syncing with iTunes" in Chapter 4.

3. Tap the app's price (or tap Free) and then tap Buy Now (or tap Install App).

   If you've already downloaded the app, Install or Installed appears instead of a price. If an update is available for an installed app, Update appears.

4. Enter your Apple ID and password, if requested, and then tap OK.

   The download starts. A dimmed app icon showing a progress meter appears on your Home screen. You can flick among your Home screens or open other apps during the download.

   When the download completes, the app is installed immediately. (If a download is interrupted, your iPad restarts the download when it reconnects to the Internet.)

TIP See Chapter 1 for details on managing app icons on your Home screen and on opening, switching among, and closing apps.

Updating Apps

Developers occasionally update their apps with bug fixes, new features, and other improvements, and release the new version through the store. If any updates are available, a numbered badge, denoting the number of apps to be updated, appears on App Store's icon **A**.

A The superimposed red badge means that app updates are available.

All updates go through the store; you don't have to search for them on the developers' Web sites.

To update your apps:

1. In App Store, tap Updates in the bottom toolbar **B**.

   A list of updated apps appears.

2. (Optional) To learn more about an update, tap its icon in the list.
3. To update any single app, tap Free next to its name.

   or

   To update all your apps, tap Update All at the top of the screen.

4. Enter your Apple ID and password, if requested, and then tap OK.

   Progress meters appear on the Home-screen icons of the apps being updated. When the download completes, updates are installed immediately.

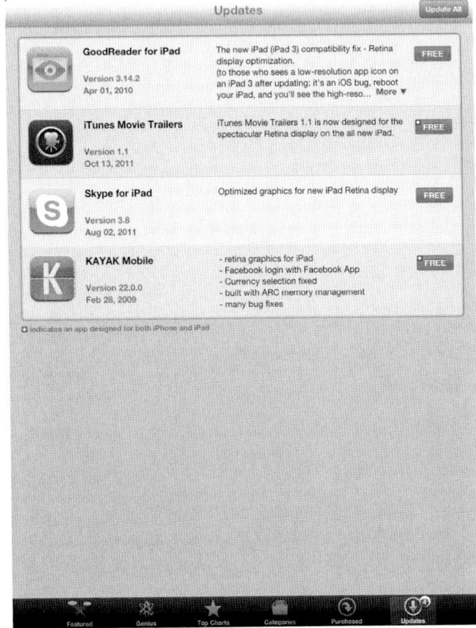

B Updates are always free. You may want to wait a few days before installing a complex or crucial app and then scan the recent reviews to make sure that the update is trouble-free.

Deleting and Reinstalling Apps

If you don't want an App Store app, you can delete it from your iPad. Deleting an app also delete all the data and documents associated with the app; to back them up, see the iCloud and iTunes sections in Chapter 4. You can't delete built-in apps.

To delete an app:

1. On the Home screen, touch and hold the app's icon until it wiggles and a badge appears in its corner.

   The badge won't appear on built-in apps.

2. Tap ⊗ and then tap Delete.
3. Click the Home button.

To reinstall an app:

1. In App Store, tap Purchased in the bottom toolbar.
2. Find the app in the list and then tap next to its name.

Changing App Settings

Many apps keep their options within the app itself; you reach them by tapping Options, Tools, or something similar while you're using the app. Some apps, however, have a separate set of options that you can access in the Settings app. To set these options, tap Settings, flick to the bottom of the left column to the list of individual apps (below Apps), and then tap the name of the app whose options you want to change Ⓐ.

TIP If you're running a small-screen app created for the iPhone or iPod touch, you can scale it up to double size to run on your iPad's big screen. Open the app and then tap the 2X button in the bottom-right corner of the screen. Scaled-up apps look blocky (pixelated). If this effect distracts you, go back to actual size by tapping 1X.

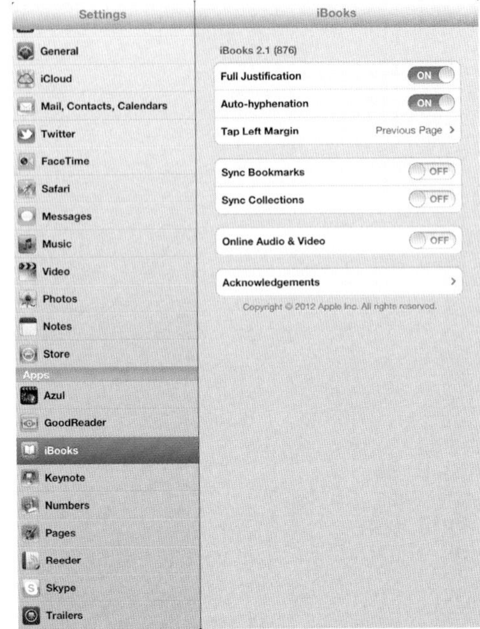

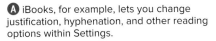

Ⓐ iBooks, for example, lets you change justification, hyphenation, and other reading options within Settings.

6

Calendar

Calendar keeps you on schedule and lets you track your life's important events. Use it to:

- View individual calendars or multiple color-coded calendars at the same time.
- View, search, and edit recent and upcoming events, and add new events.
- View events and birthdays by day, week, month, or year, or as a list.
- Set custom alerts for important events.
- Send and receive meeting invitations.
- Sync calendars by using iCloud or iTunes.
- Subscribe to calendars published online.

In This Chapter

Viewing Your Calendars

You can view calendars individually or as a single combined calendar, which makes it easy to manage work and personal calendars at the same time **A**.

TIP **Flick left or right to move from day to day, week to week, or year to year.**

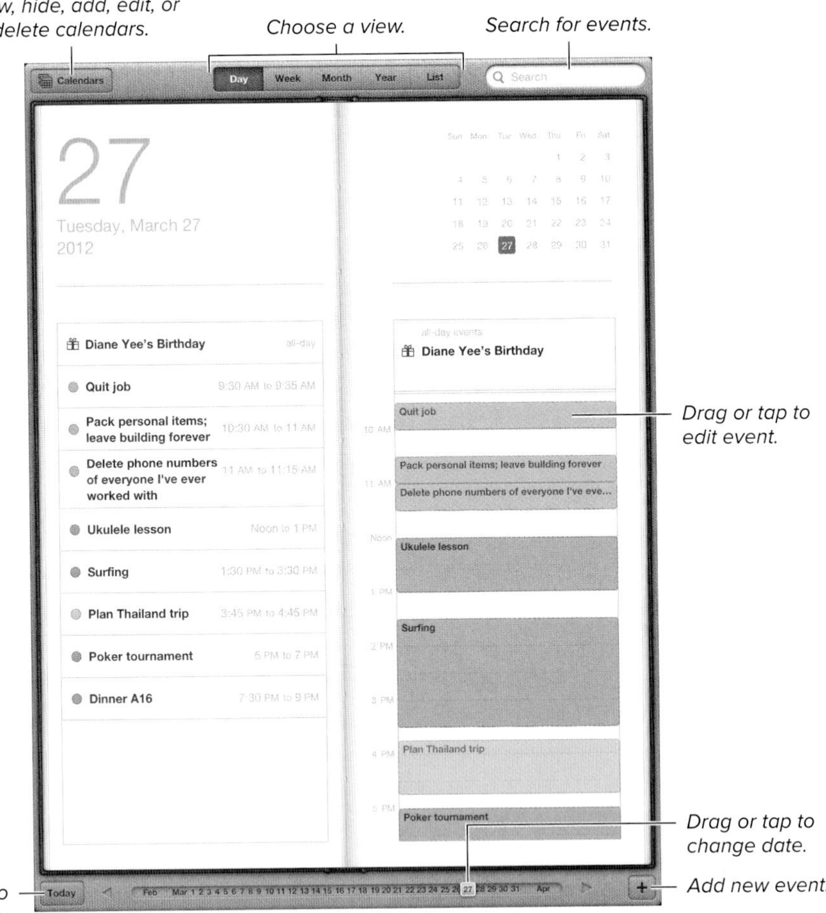

A Calendar resembles a desktop calendar, hanging wall calendar, or appointment book, depending on which view you choose.

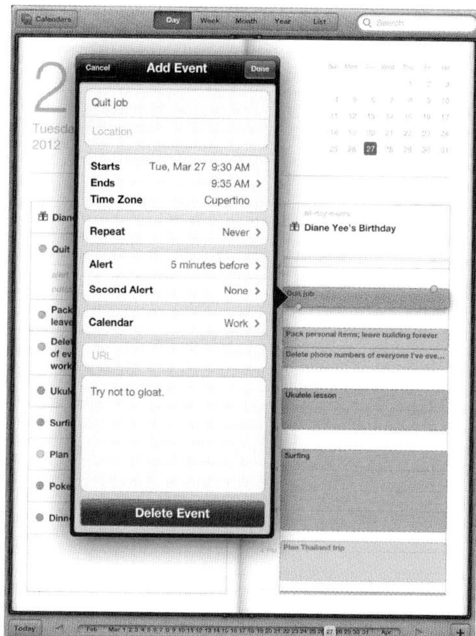

A Tapping a field shows the onscreen keyboard or specialized controls for choosing dates, times, durations, or calendars.

Adding, Editing, and Searching Events

You can add, update, delete, and search for events on any of your calendars, and set Calendar to alert you to upcoming events.

To add an event:

- Tap **+**, enter the event information, and then tap Done **A**.

  The event appears on whichever calendar you selected.

TIP To set the default calendar for events, tap Settings > Mail, Contacts, Calendars > Default Calendar.

Viewing Online Calendars

Calendar also lets you view the online calendars of people who have published them on the Internet. You can subscribe to iCalendar (.ics) or CalDAV calendars, including iCloud, Yahoo, Google, and iCal/Calendar for OS X calendars. You can read events from subscribed calendars, but you can't add or edit events. To subscribe to a calendar, tap Settings > Mail, Contacts, Calendars > Add Account > Other > Add Subscribed Calendar (or Add CalDAV Account).

You can also subscribe to Web calendars by tapping a link to the calendar in Safari. Open Safari, go to a site such as http://icalshare.com, find a calendar that you like (holidays, sports schedules, movie releases, and so on), and then tap Subscribe to Calendar. The new calendar is added to your subscription list, and its events appear in Calendar. To show or hide those dates, tap the Calendars button.

To edit or delete a calendar subscription, tap Settings > Mail, Contacts, Calendars > Subscribed Calendars.

If you ever get an iCalendar (.ics) file attached to an email message, you can tap the attachment in Mail to import its events into Calendar.

To set up alerts for events:

- To set the default alert time for events, tap Settings > Mail, Contacts, Calendars > Default Alert Times.

  or

  To make alerts appear as notifications, tap Settings > Notifications > Calendar > Notifications Center > On. (For details, see "Getting Notifications" in Chapter 4.)

  or

  To play audio alerts, tap Settings > General > Sounds > Calendar Alerts. (If your iPad is turned off, a text alert appears when you turn it on, but audio doesn't play.)

To edit an event:

1. Tap the event.
2. If a small summary window opens, tap Edit **B**.
3. In the Edit window, change the event information.

   The Edit window is the same as the Add Event window **A**.
4. Tap Done.

TIP To change an event's time or duration quickly, touch and hold the event to select it, and then drag it to a new time, or drag the grab points (small circles) to change its duration.

To delete an event:

1. Tap the event.
2. Tap Edit (if necessary).
3. Scroll to the bottom of the Edit window, and tap Delete Event **A**.

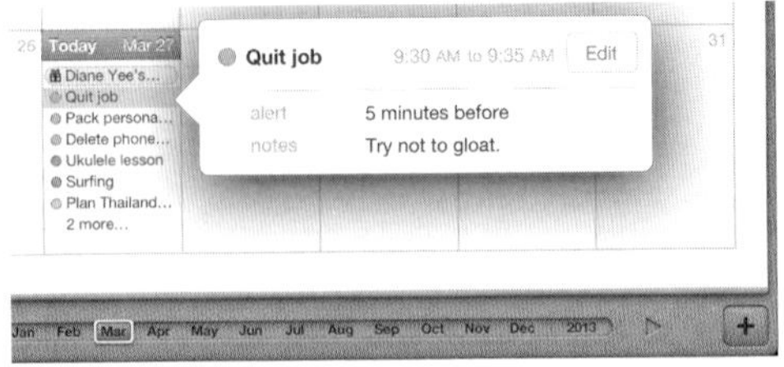

B In Week or Month view, tapping an event pops open a small summary window. Tap Edit to show the full-size Edit window.

Time Zone Support

By using Time Zone Support, you can make Calendar display event dates and times in a specific time zone or, if you're traveling, your current time zone.

To set up Time Zone Support, tap Settings > Mail, Contacts, Calendars > Time Zone Support. When Time Zone Support is turned on, Calendar displays event dates and times in the time zone that you set for the event. When Time Zone Support is turned off, Calendar displays events in the time zone of your current location as determined by your Internet connection. (For details, see "Using Location Services" in Chapter 3.)

When you're traveling, Calendar may not have enough location data to display events or alerts at the correct local time. To set the time manually, tap Settings > General > Date & Time.

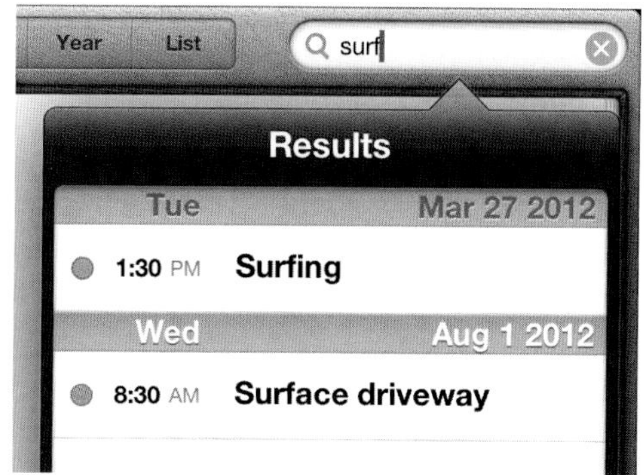

C As you type, a Results window opens to show matching events.

To search for events:

1. Tap the Search field in the top-right corner of the screen and then type one or more keywords.

   Calendar searches the events for the calendars that you're currently viewing. You can search the titles, invitees, locations, and notes fields of events.

   To clear the Search field, tap ⊗ in that field.

2. Tap an event in the Results window C.

   If necessary, flick up or down to scroll the window. If too many events are listed, you can redo your search by adding or refining keywords in the Search field.

TIP You can also search for Calendar events from the Home screen. See "Searching Your iPad" in Chapter 2.

Meeting Invitations

If you have an iCloud, Microsoft Exchange (Outlook), or CalDAV account (such as Google Calendar), you can send and receive meeting invitations. If you're using iCloud, tap Settings > iCloud > Calendars > On. To add or edit other accounts, tap Settings > Mail, Contacts, Calendars > Accounts.

To invite others to an event, tap Invitees while you're adding or editing an event and then type a name or tap ⊕ to select people from Contacts.

When you receive an invitation, it lands in the scheduled slot on your calendar with a dotted line around the event. To respond, tap the event or tap [icon] at the top of the screen to list your pending invitations. You can view the event organizer's contact info, see other invitees, add comments to your reply, or set your availability during the meeting time.

If you get a meeting invitations via email instead, tap the Invite icon attached to the message to open it and respond to the sender. If you accept, the event is added to your calendar.

To toggle alerts for new invitations, tap Settings > Mail, Contacts, Calendars > New Invitation Alerts.

Syncing Calendars

When you have multiple devices, you can use iCloud to sync your calendars across them. Update your schedule in one place and see your changes everywhere. For details, see "Using iCloud" in Chapter 4.

To sync your calendars across all your computers and iDevices, tap Settings > iCloud > Calendar > On. To sync past events, tap Settings > Mail, Contacts, Calendars > Sync (below Calendars). Future events are always synced.

Syncing Calendars in iTunes

Alternatively, you can sync with iTunes on your computer. (Pick one—don't sync calendars with *both* iCloud and iTunes.) To sync, connect your iPad to your computer (unless it's already connected with Wi-Fi Sync), click your iPad in the iTunes sidebar (on the left side), click the Info tab, and then set sync options. When you're done, click Apply or Sync.

iTunes also supports calendars for Outlook for Windows, Entourage for OS X, and iCal/Calendar for OS X. For details, see "Syncing with iTunes" in Chapter 4.

7

Camera

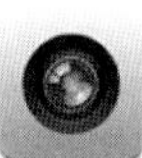

If you have an iPad 2 or later, you can use the Camera app to take still photos and record videos. Your iPad has a camera on the back, as well as a lower-quality (VGA) front camera for self-portraits and FaceTime calls (see Chapter 9). After you take photos and videos, you can view them in the Photos app (see Chapter 19), where you can also edit, share, and print them.

In This Chapter

Using the Camera Controls

Its large slab screen makes the iPad an unwieldy camera, but you can use the Camera app to take photos and record video **A**.

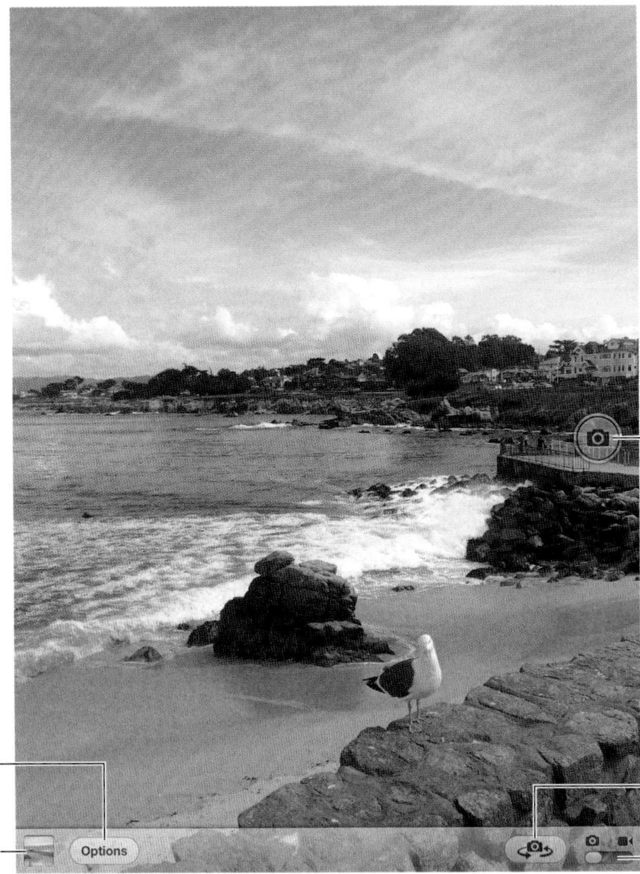
Take a photo or start/stop video recording.
Overlay a 3×3 grid to help compose the shot.
Options
View photos and videos that you've taken.
Swap front and back cameras.
Switch between photos and video.

A Camera controls.

Before You Shoot

A few tips before you shoot:

- When you take a photo or start a video recording, Camera makes a shutter sound. You can control the volume by using the volume buttons or side switch. (In some countries, the shutter sound can't be muted because of privacy laws.)
- You can hold the iPad vertically or horizontally to shoot. Portrait (tall) videos get letterboxed when they're played on some sharing Web sites.
- To view new photos and videos, tap Photos > Albums > Camera Roll. A thumbnail of the most recent shot also appears in the bottom-left corner of the Camera screen; tap it to jump to the photo or video in the Camera Roll album. You can also flick the screen from left to right to see it.
- If Location Services (see Chapter 3) is turned on for Camera, photos and videos are tagged with location data that can be used by photo-related apps and photo-sharing Web sites.
- If Photo Stream is turned on (to do so, tap Settings > iCloud), new photos also appear in your Photo Stream album in the Photos app, and are streamed to your other iOS devices and computers. See "Using iCloud" in Chapter 4.

Taking Photos and Recording Video

Taking photos and videos with your iPad is little different from taking them with an iPhone or a point-and-shoot camera.

To take a photo:

1. Set the Camera/Video switch to [camera icon].
2. Line up the shot.

   Camera autofocuses, or you can tap to focus (iPad 3 or later).
3. Tap [shutter icon], or press the Volume Up button.

   To prevent blurry photos, which can result when you tap [shutter icon] too hard, touch and hold the icon while you line up your shot, and lift your finger when you're ready to take the photo.

TIP When you photograph people (or animals), the iPad 3 or later uses face detection to automatically focus on and balance the exposure across up to ten faces. A rectangle appears over each detected face.

To record a video:

1. Set the Camera/Video switch to ■◀.
2. Line up the shot.

   Camera autofocuses, or you can tap to focus (iPad 3 or later).
3. Tap ●, or press the Volume Up button.

   The timer in the top-right corner of the screen shows the current length of the video. The microphone on the top-center edge of the iPad records the audio.
4. Tap or press again to stop recording.

TIP You can also take screen shots of whatever is on your iPad's screen (like the figures in this book). To do so, press and release the Sleep/Wake button and the Home button at the same time. The screen flashes, and the screen shot is added to your Camera Roll album (or, on an iPad 1, to your Saved Photos album).

Using Photo and Video Tools

Camera offers photo and video tools for use before and after the shot.

Overlaying a grid. Tap Options to toggle a 3×3 overlay on the screen **A**. This grid helps you compose a photo by using the "rule of thirds" guideline, which states that important compositional elements should be placed along the gridlines or their intersections. The grid doesn't appear for video.

continues on next page

A Camera tools help you compose your photo before you take the shot.

Zooming in or out. Pinch the screen to show the zoom slider A. Drag the slider left or right to zoom out or in, or pinch or spread two fingers on the screen to zoom. Zoom works for the back camera only and not for video.

Adjusting the exposure. The iPad lacks a flash, but it lets you adjust the exposure (overall lightness) of a photo. When you line up the shot, tap a person, object, or any other area of the screen. A blue-white square appears briefly as Camera focuses and adjusts the exposure based on that area A. To lock the exposure, touch and hold an area until the square pulses and then lift your finger; the text *AE/AF Lock* appears at the bottom of the screen (until you tap again). Now take the photo or video.

Editing photos. To edit a photo, open the Photos app, view the photo full-screen, tap the screen to show the controls, tap Edit, and then tap an editing tool at the bottom of the screen B:

- Tap Rotate to spin the photo in 90-degree increments.
- Tap Enhance to improve contrast, color saturation, and other qualities automatically.
- Tap Red-Eye and then tap each eye to correct it.
- Tap Crop, drag the corners of the grid (or tap Constrain to set a grid ratio), drag the photo to reposition it, and then tap Crop in the top-right corner.

When you're done editing, tap the buttons at the top of the screen to cancel, undo, or save your edits.

TIP For heavy-duty photo editing, try Apple's iPhoto for iOS app, available in the App Store.

B You can rotate, enhance, remove red-eye from, and crop photos.

Drag to trim video.

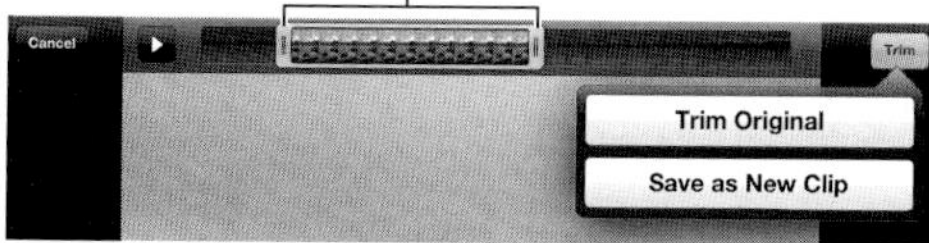

C The frame viewer turns yellow when you trim frames from the start or end of a video.

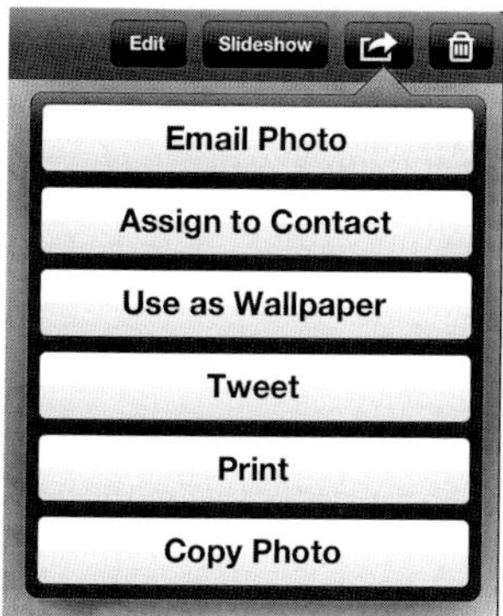

D You can share, upload, or use your photos and videos in various ways.

Trimming videos. To trim a video, open the Photos app, view the video full-screen, and then tap the screen to show the controls **C**. Drag either end of the frame viewer to trim the frames from the start or end of a video. Tap Trim Original to replace the original video (permanently deleting trimmed frames), or tap Save as New Clip to save the trimmed version and leave the original video unaffected.

TIP To turn your videos into Hollywood-style movies, try Apple's iMovie for iOS app, available in the App Store.

Sharing, viewing, and printing. Open the Photos app, view the photo or video full-screen, tap the screen to show the controls, and then tap [share icon] **D**. You can email or copy photos and videos, upload videos to YouTube, tweet or print photos, and more. To delete a photo or video, tap [trash icon].

To transfer photos and videos to your computer:

1. Connect your iPad to your Mac or Windows PC.
2. Choose the Import command in your photo-organizer program (iPhoto, Windows Live Photo Gallery, or whatever) to copy your photo and video files to the computer.

8

Contacts

Contacts, an electronic address book, stores names, addresses, telephone numbers, email addresses, birthdays, and other contact information. Your contacts are available in Mail, Messages, FaceTime, Calendar, and other apps and services that tap into Contacts. You can add contacts by typing them manually or by syncing with other lists of contacts.

In This Chapter

Adding and Editing Contacts

Contacts resembles a physical address book **A**. On the left page, browse contacts by tapping, flicking, or searching. On the right page, scroll contact info, or tap a field or button to call, email, send a message, video-chat, share a vCard (.vcf) file, show an address in Maps, open a home page, and more.

TIP To change how contacts are sorted and displayed, and to designate your own contact info, tap Settings > Mail, Contacts, Calendars > Contacts. To set the default ringtone and text tone, tap Settings > General > Sounds.

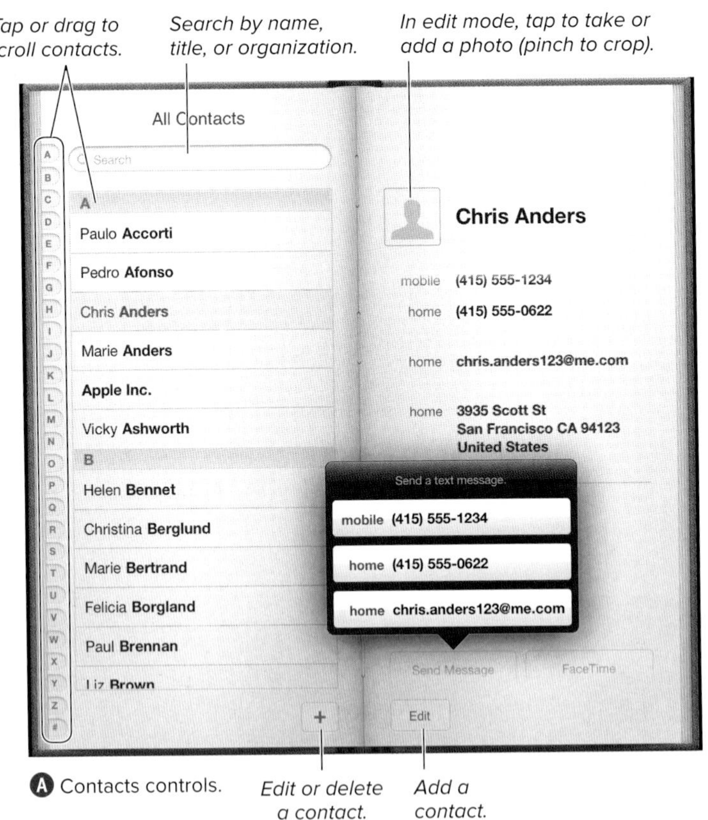

A Contacts controls.

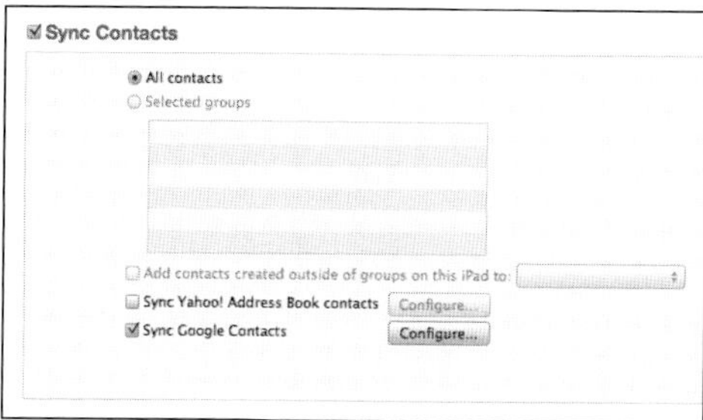

Ⓐ You can use iTunes to sync Contacts with contacts lists in popular email and address-book programs and services.

Syncing Contacts

Besides adding contacts directly on your iPad, you can sync with other contacts lists:

- **iCloud.** To sync contacts wirelessly across your devices, tap Settings > iCloud > Contacts > On. For details, see "Using iCloud" in Chapter 4.
- **iTunes on your computer.** Connect your iPad to your computer via USB cable or Wi-Fi Sync, click your iPad in the iTunes sidebar (on the left), click the Info tab, and then set Sync Contacts options Ⓐ. When you're done, click Apply or Sync. iTunes supports contacts for Outlook, Entourage, Windows Contacts, OS X Contacts, Address Book, Yahoo Address Book, Google Contacts, and more. For some programs, you must first turn on sync or sharing services in the program itself; look for a setting in the Preferences or Options dialog box. Don't sync contacts with *both* iCloud and iTunes. For details, see "Syncing with iTunes" in Chapter 4.
- **Work or school directories.** Contacts supports Microsoft Exchange (GAL), LDAP, and CardDAV servers. To add a Contacts account, tap Settings > Mail, Contacts, Calendars > Add Account. Configure the account based on information you get from your network administrator or organization's IT department. When you sync with an external directory, a Groups button appears at the top of the Contacts screen; tap Groups to change directories. You can't add or edit contacts in GAL, LDAP, or CardDAV contacts lists, but you can copy a contact to your personal list by tapping Add Contact.

9

FaceTime

Use FaceTime to make video calls over Wi-Fi. (A cellular connection won't work.) The other caller must have an iPhone, iPad, or iPod touch with a forward-facing camera, or a camera-equipped Mac running FaceTime for OS X.

In This Chapter

Making a FaceTime Call

FaceTime identifies you by your Apple ID and is integrated with Contacts (see Chapter 8). To make a FaceTime call, you choose someone from your contacts or favorites, or list of recent calls. A simple set of controls appears onscreen while you chat **A**.

TIP To set the options for FaceTime, tap Settings > FaceTime. To be notified of missed calls, tap Settings > Notifications > FaceTime.

A FaceTime controls.

When you open FaceTime, you may be prompted to sign in with your Apple ID or to create a new account.

To make a FaceTime call:

1. In FaceTime, tap Favorites, Recents, or Contacts at the bottom of the screen.
2. Tap the name, phone number, or email address of the person you want to call.

   You can use the controls at the top of the screen to add favorites, add contacts, and edit the lists.
3. After the other party accepts the call, you can do any of the following:
   - **Drag your image.** Drag the picture-in-picture image to any corner (A), if it's in the way.
   - **Mute the call.** Tap [mute icon] to temporarily turn off sound. You can still hear and see the caller, and he or she can see but not hear you. Tap [mute icon] again to unmute.
   - **Swap cameras.** Tap [swap cameras icon] to swap cameras to talk face to face (front camera) or show the caller what's around you (back camera). The inset image shows you what the caller is seeing.
   - **Change screen orientation.** Rotate your iPad to portrait (tall) or landscape (wide) view. To lock rotation, see "Changing Screen Orientation" in Chapter 1.
   - **Switch apps.** Press the Home button and then tap an app icon. You and the caller can still talk, but you can't see each other. To return to the call, tap the green bar at the top of the screen.
4. When you're done talking, tap End to end the call.

10

Game Center

Game Center lets you play games on Apple's online multiplayer social gaming network, which Apple says has more than 100 million members around the world. You can get Game Center–compatible games from the App Store to play against friends or strangers on iPhones, iPads, iPods, or Macs.

Game Center offers features common to most gaming networks. You can add people to your friends list or receive friend requests from others. Friends can invite each other to play or find equally matched opponents. You can earn bonus points for games that reward points for completing certain tasks, and you can see what your friends have achieved. Game leaderboards rank the best players.

In This Chapter

Setting Up a Game Center Account

To use Game Center, you need an Internet connection and an Apple ID. If you like, you can create a separate Apple ID for gaming and still use your main Apple ID for iCloud, App Store, iTunes, and so on.

The first time you sign in to Game Center, you must create a nickname, which is your unique user name in Game Center **A**. You can change your nickname at any time in account settings, but only one nickname at a time can be associated with an Apple ID. Other players can search for you by using your nickname. Account settings also let you configure privacy-related options, such as whether to accept game invitations or display your real name.

Some Game Center settings are in the Settings app. To be notified of friend requests and game invitations, tap Settings > Notifications > Game Center. To block friend requests or disable multiplayer activity, tap Settings > General > Restrictions > Game Center.

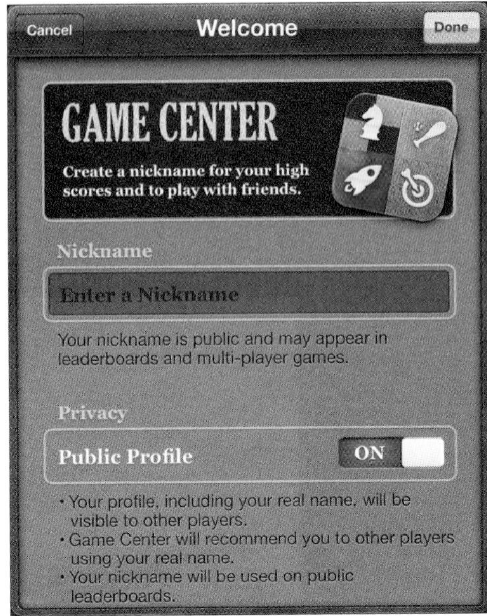

A If you pick a nickname that someone is already using, Game Center suggests alternatives, which you're free to ignore. If you see your nickname at the top of the Me screen, you're already signed in.

Ⓐ The Me screen is festooned with the icons of the popular Game Center games. Tap an icon to view its Info screen.

Using Game Center

After you sign in, tap the buttons in the bottom toolbar to edit your account, play or buy games, or manage your friends:

Me. View or buy top games; add or take a photo (pinch and drag to crop); declare your status, which you define; view or edit your account settings (tap Account banner > View Account); or sign out (tap Account banner > Sign Out) Ⓐ.

TIP You don't need to sign out each time you quit Game Center.

Friends. Invite people or contacts to be friends, get friend recommendations, invite friends to play, see games that friends play, buy a game that a friend has, check a friend's scores, search your friends list, list a friend's friends, remove (unfriend) a friend, or report problems or cheaters.

TIP No friends? Unresponsive friends? Tap Auto-Match to have Game Center find another player for you.

continues on next page

Games. Play a game, get game recommendations, search for Game Center games, tell a friend about a game, view leaderboards (rankings) and achievements, or get a game from the App Store **B**. (Not all Game Center–compatible games feature multiplayer play.)

TIP To find Game Center games from within App Store, tap App Store > Categories > Games, scroll to the bottom of the screen, and then tap Game Center (below Quick Links).

Requests. Invite people to be friends, respond to friend requests, or search for requests.

TIP Apple maintains and updates your Game Center profile automatically. Your profile contains your nickname, friends list, achievement points, photo, status, Game Center–compatible games owned, and more.

B Tap a game on the Games screen to see its Info screen, which includes leaderboards and achievements.

Turn-Based Games

In many multiplayer games—racing and cooperative games being obvious examples—all players play at the same time. Other games—particularly board and card games such as backgammon, Scrabble, and poker—are *turn-based,* in that each player waits until the other acts before proceeding. Game Center keeps track of each player's turn and can manage multiple games if you're playing more than one. If it's taking a long time between moves, Game Center can notify you when it's your turn in Notification Center. To get notifications (see Chapter 4), tap Settings > Notifications > Game Center.

Some games have several modes of play: online in Game Center, on two different iPads over the same Wi-Fi or Bluetooth connection, or face-to-face by passing the iPad back and forth. To find these games, search for *multiplayer* in the App Store (Chapter 5). One example is the high-priced version of Scrabble.

iBooks

iBooks is Apple's free e-book reader for the iPad, iPhone, and iPod touch. Like the Amazon Kindle and other e-readers, iBooks lets you download books and read them onscreen. iBooks isn't a built-in app; to install it, tap App Store, search for *ibooks,* and then download the app. (For App Store details, see Chapter 5.)

In This Chapter

Stocking Your Library

You can stock your library by downloading books from the iBookstore (Apple's online bookstore) or adding books that you've downloaded from the Internet. After you've added books to your library, you don't need an Internet connection to read them. iBooks lets you read books in EPUB and PDF formats—the two most popular free and open e-book standards.

You can choose among hundreds of thousands of free and paid titles in the iBookstore. To download books from the iBookstore, you need an Apple ID and a wireless Internet connection (Wi-Fi or cellular). You can browse and search books, read reviews, buy a book, or get one of the many free books. A downloaded book automatically adds itself to your iBooks library, where you can start reading it immediately. Before you buy a book, you can read other readers' ratings and reviews or download a free sample of the book's content.

A The Featured screen shows new and notable books spotlighted by Apple's iBookstore staff. Flick to the bottom of the screen to see special groups of books, such as books made into movies, limited-time offers, and popular preorders.

To shop in the iBookstore:

1. Open iBooks.
2. If you're reading a book, tap the center of the screen to show the reading controls and then tap Library in the top-left corner of the page.
3. Tap Store in the top-left corner of the library.

   The iBookstore opens.
4. To browse for books, tap one of the buttons at the bottom of the screen (Featured, Top Charts, and so on) **A**.

   or

   To search for a book, tap the Search field at the top of the screen and then type a book title or author name.

B A book's Info screen shows the book description, standard book data (price, title, publisher, author, and so on), customer ratings and reviews, and links to related material.

5. To display detailed information about a book, tap the book's cover.

   The book's Info screen appears **B**.

6. Tap one of the buttons below the cover image to buy the book, get a free sample, or download a free book.

   The iBookstore spins to display your library bookshelf, puts your book on the top shelf, and then shows a progress bar that tracks the download.

7. When the download completes, tap the book's cover to read it.

TIP To quickly download a book that you bought and deleted or bought on another iDevice, tap Purchased at the bottom of the iBookstore screen. To sync your book purchases across all your iDevices automatically, tap Settings > Store > Books > On (below Automatic Downloads). For details, see "Using iCloud" in Chapter 4.

Free Books from the Internet

The Internet is stuffed with free books in EPUB and PDF formats, which you can download and add to your iBooks library.

Much of what's freely available is in the public domain (not covered by intellectual-property rights). Public-domain works in EPUB and other formats are available by the millions in Internet libraries, including Google Books (http://books.google.com), Internet Archive (http://archive.org), ManyBooks.net (http://manybooks.net), Open Library (http://openlibrary.org), and Project Gutenberg (www.gutenberg.org).

To add downloaded books to your iBooks library, connect your iPad to your computer via USB cable or Wi-Fi Sync, click Books below your iPad in the iTunes sidebar (on the left side), and then drag book files from a folder window to the Books list in iTunes.

You can also download books directly to your iBooks library. On your iPad, open Safari; go to any site that provides EPUB or PDF books; tap the download link for the book; and then open the book in iBooks. This technique also works in other apps. If you receive a book (or book link) via email or Dropbox, for example, tap it to add the book to your library.

Viewing and Organizing Your Library

Books downloaded from the iBookstore or the Internet appear in your iBooks library. You can organize your library by rearranging, sorting, categorizing, and deleting books. You can access your library at any time from the iBookstore or while you're reading a book.

For most maintenance tasks, you use the library toolbar at the top of the screen.

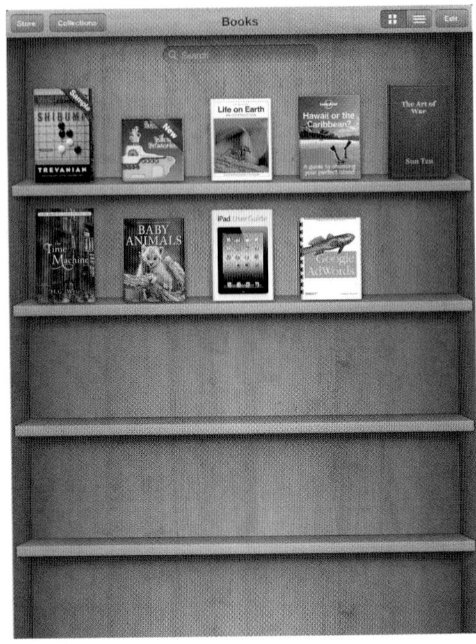

Ⓐ An iBooks library in bookshelf view...

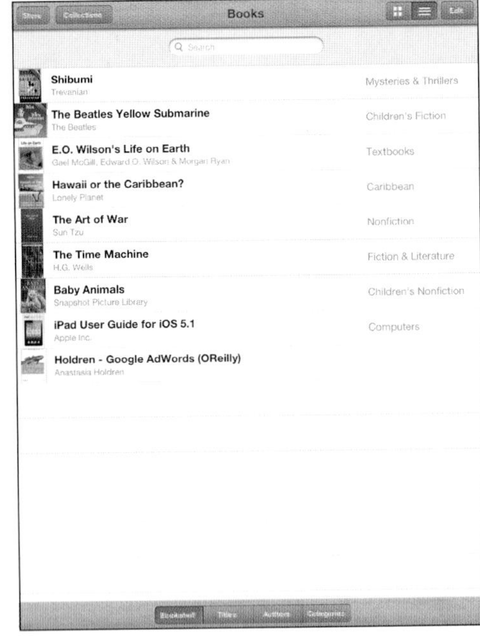

Ⓑ ...and in list view.

To view your library:

- If you're in the iBookstore, tap Library in the top-left corner of the screen.

  or

  If you're reading a book, tap the center of the screen to show the reading controls and then tap Library in the top-left corner of the page.

To organize your library:

- **Change the view.** In bookshelf view, iBooks shows the front covers of your books on virtual wooden bookshelves. In list view, your books appear as a sortable list of titles, authors, subjects, and thumbnail cover images. Bookshelf view Ⓐ is pretty, but list view Ⓑ is more practical for managing a large library. To change views, tap a view button at the right end of the toolbar.
- **Rearrange books.** In bookshelf view Ⓐ, touch and hold a book until it rises out of the bookshelf, and then drag it to a new position. In list view Ⓑ, tap the Bookshelf button at the bottom of the screen, tap Edit in the toolbar, and then

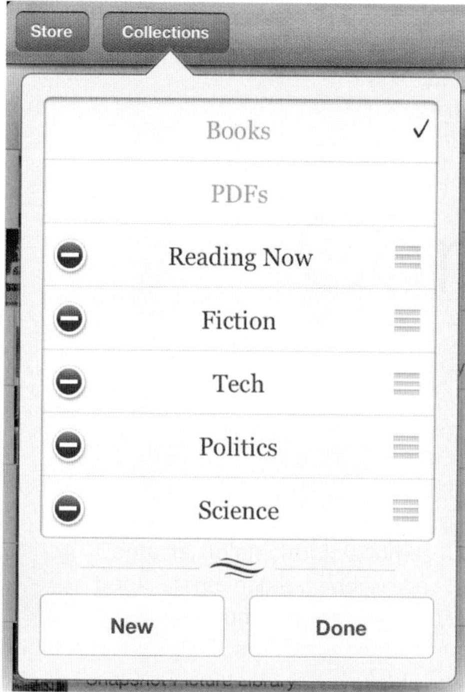

C You can organize your books in custom categories.

drag the grabber handles ☰ to reorder the books. To sort books in list view, tap one of the buttons at the bottom of the screen.

- **Create collections.** You can organize your books in *collections* on topics of your choosing (by author, by genre, and so on). iBooks comes with two built-in generic collections—Books and PDFs—and you can create, view, edit, and delete others. To do so, tap Collections in the toolbar **C**. Your collections appear as separate library screens that you can switch to or cycle through by tapping Collections. In bookshelf view **A**, you can flick left or right on the bookshelf to cycle through collections. To move a book to a different collection, tap Edit in the toolbar. Deleting a collection deletes the books in that collection. You can't edit or delete the built-in Books and PDFs collections, however.

TIP To back up your collections when you sync, tap Settings, tap iBooks (on the left), and then turn on Sync Collections.

- **Delete books.** To delete a book, view the collection containing the book. Tap Edit in the toolbar, tap the target book(s), and then tap Delete.
- **Search for books.** You can search for library books by title or author. To do so in any collection or view, flick down to reveal the Search field at the top of the screen, tap the Search field, and then type the book title or author name.

Reading Books

To open a book, tap its cover in your library. The first time you open a book, the first page appears (or one of the early pages appears, depending on the publisher's settings). If you open a book that you've been reading, it opens to the page where you left off. You can rotate your iPad to read in portrait (one-page) or landscape (two-page) view.

iBooks shows a clean page with no distracting elements. Turning a page requires only a tap on the screen edge, but for some tasks, you must summon the reading controls and page navigator by tapping the center of the screen **A**.

TIP In addition to supporting EPUB and PDF books, iBooks supports textbooks that include normal text interspersed with interactive high-quality images, sounds, videos, animations, and 3D objects. You can find interactive textbooks in the Textbooks category of the iBookstore. These textbooks use a proprietary iBooks-only Apple format. For a taste, download *Life on Earth,* a free biology textbook by E.O. Wilson.

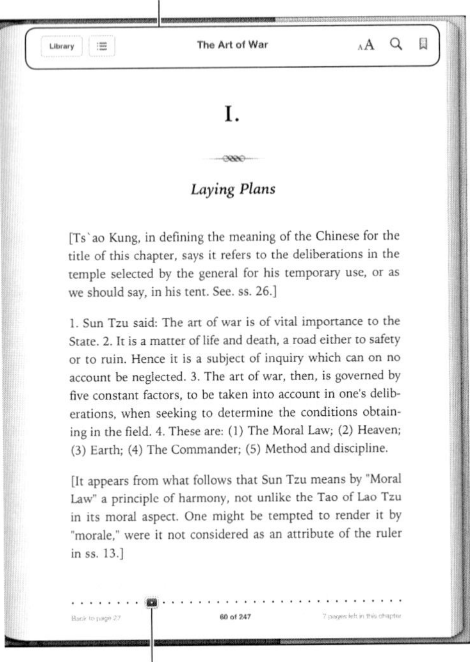

Reading controls
Library
The Art of War
AA
I.
Laying Plans
[Ts`ao Kung, in defining the meaning of the Chinese for the title of this chapter, says it refers to the deliberations in the temple selected by the general for his temporary use, or as we should say, in his tent. See. ss. 26.]
1. Sun Tzu said: The art of war is of vital importance to the State. 2. It is a matter of life and death, a road either to safety or to ruin. Hence it is a subject of inquiry which can on no account be neglected. 3. The art of war, then, is governed by five constant factors, to be taken into account in one's deliberations, when seeking to determine the conditions obtaining in the field. 4. These are: (1) The Moral Law; (2) Heaven; (3) Earth; (4) The Commander; (5) Method and discipline.
[It appears from what follows that Sun Tzu means by "Moral Law" a principle of harmony, not unlike the Tao of Lao Tzu in its moral aspect. One might be tempted to render it by "morale," were it not considered as an attribute of the ruler in ss. 13.]
Back to page 27
60 of 247
7 pages left in this chapter
Page navigator

A A book open in portrait view. To show or hide the reading controls and page navigator, tap the center of the screen.

Using the iBooks Controls

You can do any of the following things while you read, using the reading controls or page navigator:

Turn the page. To flip to the next page, tap the right side of the screen (or flick left to right). To flip to the previous page, tap the left side of the screen (or flick to the right to left).

Jump to a page. To jump to an arbitrary page, drag the slider on the page navigator. To jump to a specific page number, tap and then type a page number. To jump by chapter, flick left or right with three fingers. To jump to a specific chapter or section, tap.

Revisit a page. To revisit a page that you've seen recently, tap the Back to Page or Go to Page link at the bottom of the screen.

Enlarge an image. To enlarge an image, double-tap the image. Double-tap again to resume reading.

Bookmark a page. Tap to bookmark a page that you want to return to. It's unnecessary to bookmark your current page when you close a book, because iBooks remembers where you left off. To see all your bookmarks, tap.

Annotate text. Touch and hold any word, and then drag over text to highlight it. Use the pop-up menu to change the highlight color, switch to underlining, remove the highlight, or add or edit a note. To see all your highlights and notes, tap.

TIP To back up your bookmarks, highlights, and notes when you sync, tap Settings > iBooks and then turn on Sync Bookmarks.

continues on next page

Change the type and layout. Tap AA to change the screen brightness, text size, font, or theme (text and background color). To eliminate the visual clutter at the edges of the screen (the fake pages, spine, and cover edges), tap Theme and then turn on Full Screen.

TIP To justify or hyphenate text, tap Settings > iBooks and then toggle Full Justification or Auto-hyphenation.

Use text tools. To search in a book, tap Q and then type a word or phrase. To define a word, double-tap the word and then tap Define in the pop-up menu. To copy text, double-tap a word to select it, drag the blue drag points to encompass the target text, and then tap Copy in the pop-up menu. You can paste the text into another app.

Close the book. To shut the book and return to your bookshelf, tap Library in the top-left corner of the screen.

Managing PDFs

When you add a PDF file to your library, iBooks places it in the PDFs collection and adds a comb binding to its cover image to distinguish it from EPUB books.

Many of the methods that you use to read EPUBs also apply to PDFs. To email or print a PDF (which you can't do to an EPUB file), tap . You can't select or copy text, add highlights or notes, or use the built-in dictionary in a PDF.

If you read a lot of PDFs, you may prefer GoodReader, available in the App Store.

12

iTunes, Music, and Videos

iTunes is the gateway to Apple's online iTunes Store, where you can download music, movies, TV shows, and other digital content. To download from the store, you need an Apple ID and a Internet connection (Wi-Fi or cellular).

Music, audiobooks, and other audio content downloaded from the iTunes Store appear automatically in the Music app, where you can play them or create playlists. You can also use Music to listen to audio ripped from CDs or downloaded from the Internet.

Movies, TV shows, and other video content downloaded from the iTunes Store appear automatically in the Videos app, which lets you watch them on your iPad or on an external display. You can also use Videos to watch videos ripped from DVDs or downloaded from the Internet.

In This Chapter

Shopping in the iTunes Store

Use iTunes to add content to your iPad. You can browse and buy music, movies, TV shows, audiobooks, and more.

To shop in the iTunes Store:

1. Open iTunes on your iPad **A**.

   The store opens to the Music screen the first time and remembers your last open screen thereafter.

2. To browse for content, tap one of the buttons at the bottom of the screen (Music, Movies, TV Shows, and so on).

   or

   To search for content, tap the Search field at the top of the screen and then type an artist, actor, title, or other keyword.

TIP The buttons at the top of the screen let you see featured content, top sellers, or Genius recommendations. Buttons at the bottom of most iTunes Store screens let you log in or out of your Apple ID account, redeem iTunes gift cards, or get technical support for a problem.

3. To display detailed information about an item, tap the item's cover or thumbnail image.

   The item's Info screen appears **B** **C**. This screen, which varies by content type, shows items such as a description, genre, tracks, episodes, release date, ratings, reviews, links to related material, and more.

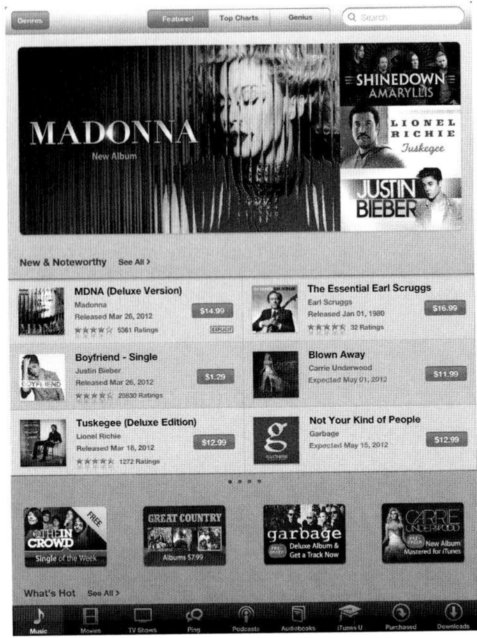

A The Music section of the iTunes Store.

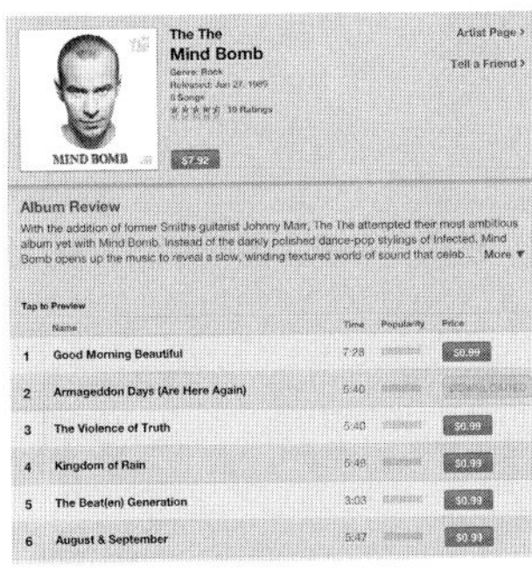

B Info screens for a music album...

C ...and for a movie.

iTunes on Your Computer

You can buy the same content from iTunes on your iPad and iTunes on your Mac or Windows PC. A few tips if you're using the latter:

- To sync iTunes Store content between your iPad and your computer, see "Syncing with iTunes" in Chapter 4.
- If you lose your Internet connection during a download, choose Store > Check for Available Downloads to resume downloading.
- Apple lets you play iTunes Store purchases on up to five computers. To authorize a computer, choose Store > Authorize Computer.
- To share media on a network, choose Advanced > Turn on Home Sharing on each of up to five computers on your network. Shared content appears in the iTunes sidebar on each computer.
- To add non–iTunes Store content (such as imported media files) to your iPad, connect your iPad to your computer via USB cable or Wi-Fi Sync and then drag the files from a folder window to your iPad in the iTunes sidebar. The Music and Videos apps accept only supported formats, such as MP3 or AAC for audio and MP4 for video. For a list of formats, see www.apple.com/ipad/specs.
- Some common video formats, such as AVI, MKV, and WMV, won't play on your iPad, but you can convert them with Apple's QuickTime Pro, Handbrake (http://handbrake.fr), or another video-conversion tool. It's easier, however, to buy an iPad video-player app that supports a wide range of formats, such as CineXPlayer or Azul Media Player.

4. To download an item, tap a price button, or tap Free.

   You can preview clips before you buy. For music, buy albums or individual tracks. For movies, buy or rent high- (HD) or standard-definition (SD) video. For TV shows, buy entire seasons/series or individual episodes.

TIP To download classes and materials from iTunes U(niversity), get the free iTunes U app from the App Store (see Chapter 5).

5. To see downloads in progress, tap Downloads at the bottom of the screen.

   When a download completes, the item lands in the Music app or the Videos app, depending on its type.

TIP To quickly download an item that you bought and deleted or bought on another iDevice, tap Purchased at the bottom of the iTunes screen. To sync your music purchases across all your iDevices automatically, tap Settings > Store > Music > On (below Automatic Downloads). For details, see "Using iCloud" in Chapter 4.

Playing Music

You can use the Music app to listen to music, audiobooks, and other audio content downloaded from the iTunes Store or copied from your computer. You can listen to audio over the built-in speaker, earphones plugged in to the headphone jack, or wireless Bluetooth headphones or speakers. The iPad's built-in speaker is silenced when you use earphones or external speakers. See also "Adjusting the Volume" in Chapter 1.

To play music or audio content:

1. Open Music.
2. Tap the buttons along the bottom of the screen (Playlist, Songs, and so on) to browse your collection.
3. To play an item, tap it.
4. Use the controls at the top of the screen to control playback **A**.

TIP To see all the tracks on the current album, switch to the Now Playing screen and then tap ☰ in the bottom-right corner. Tap a track to play it. (If the Now Playing controls aren't visible, tap the screen first.)

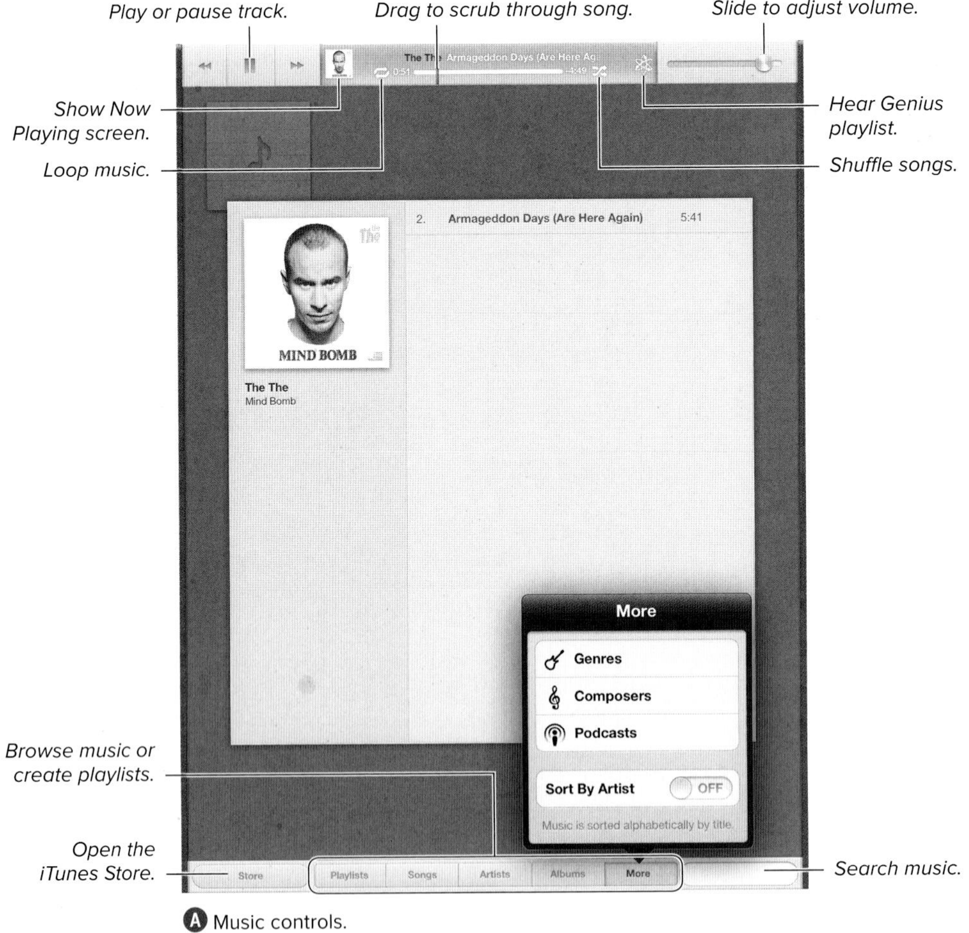

A Music controls.

B These controls operate the currently playing app, or—if the music is paused—the most recent app that played. The icon for the app appears on the right; tap it to open the app.

Music still plays when you switch to another app or when the iPad screen is locked. To show playback controls while you're using another app, double-click the Home button to show the multitasking bar at the bottom of the screen **B** and then flick left to right. Double-clicking the Home button also shows playback controls when the screen is locked.

TIP **To set other Music options, tap Settings > Music. iTunes Match is a subscription service that backs up all your music—even songs ripped from CDs or downloaded from the Internet—in iCloud. For details, see www.apple.com/itunes/itunes-match.**

Playing Videos

You can use the Videos app to watch movies, TV shows, and other video content downloaded from the iTunes Store or copied from your computer. As with Music, you can listen to audio through the built-in speaker, earphones plugged in to the headphone jack, or wireless Bluetooth headphones or speakers.

TIP To play video on an HDTV or another external display, see "Streaming with AirPlay" and "Screen Mirroring" in Chapter 3.

Playback Tips

Here are a few tips to improve video playback on your iPad:

- To speed backward or forward, touch and hold ⏮ or ⏭.
- If the video's scenes are demarcated by chapter markers, tap ⏮ or ⏭ to jump to the previous or next chapter.
- If the video has multiple language tracks, subtitles, or closed captioning, tap 💬 to control those features.
- Double-tap the screen to swap between widescreen and full-screen view.
- As you drag the playback slider (scrubber), you can slide your finger down to slow the scrub rate. A label indicates *Hi-Speed Scrubbing, Half Speed Scrubbing,* and so on.
- To set other options, tap Settings > Videos.

To play movies, TV shows, or video content:

1. Open Videos.
2. Tap the buttons along the top of the screen (Movies, TV Shows, or Podcasts) to browse your collection.
3. To play an item, tap it, or tap ▶.
4. Use the onscreen controls **A** to control playback.

TIP You can rotate your iPad to watch in portrait or landscape view.

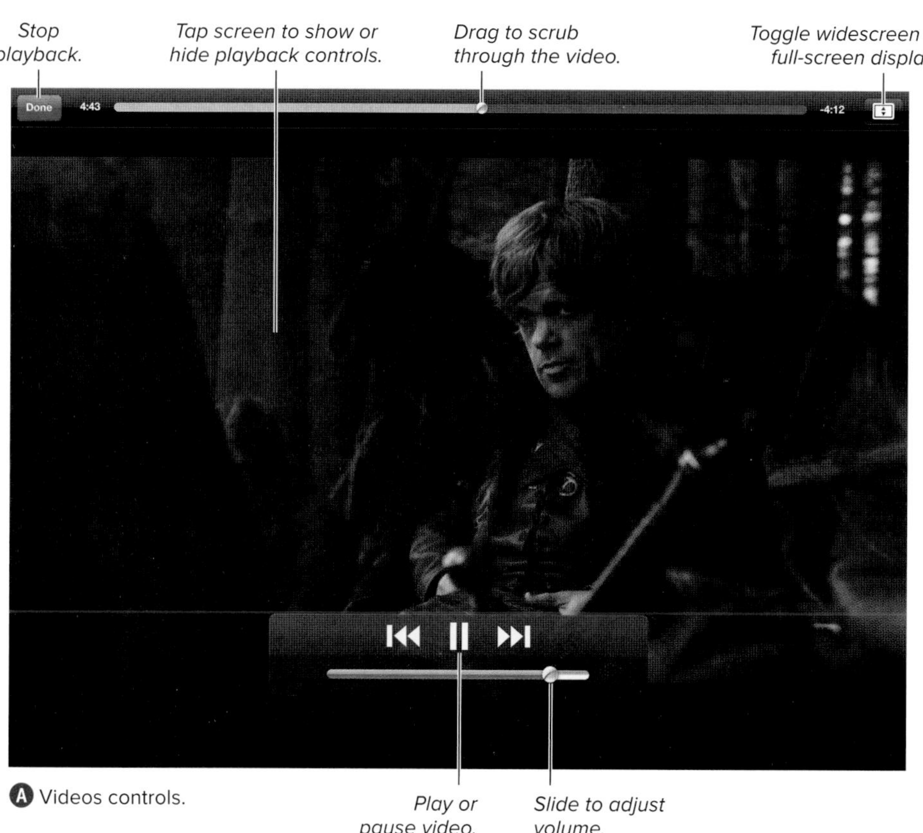

Stop playback.
Tap screen to show or hide playback controls.
Drag to scrub through the video.
Toggle widescreen and full-screen display.
Done
4:43
-4:12
Play or pause video.
Slide to adjust volume.

A Videos controls.

13

Mail

Mail is the iPad's email app. You must be connected to the Internet (Wi-Fi or cellular signal) to send or receive mail. This chapter shows you how to:

- Set up email accounts
- Read mail
- Write, format, and send mail
- Change mail settings

In This Chapter

Setting Up Email Accounts

To get your messages flowing into Mail, you must set up your email account settings so that Mail knows where to find your mailboxes on the Internet. If you're using a dedicated email program like Microsoft Outlook or Apple Mail on your computer, you can copy your account settings to your iPad via iTunes. Otherwise, you can set up your accounts directly on your iPad.

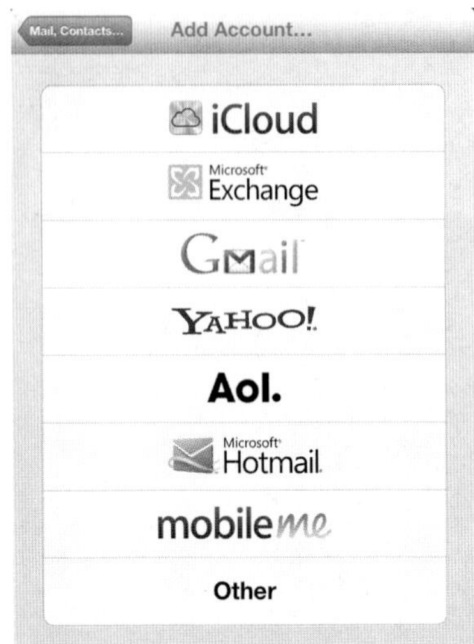

Ⓐ The Add Account screen lists the most popular Web-based mail providers, as well as Microsoft Exchange (for work or school servers).

TIP If you use a Web-based email account such as Gmail, Yahoo, or Hotmail, you don't really have to use Mail. You can open Safari, the iPad's Web browser, and then log in to and use your account normally. Some bigger services, such as Google, have their own free mail apps in the App Store (see Chapter 5).

To sync mail accounts with iTunes on your computer:

1. Connect your iPad to your computer via USB cable or Wi-Fi Sync.
2. In iTunes, click your iPad in the iTunes sidebar (on the left).
3. Click the Info tab and then set Sync Mail Accounts options.

   Select only the accounts that you want to use on your iPad.
4. When you're done, click Apply or Sync.

   Your account settings—but not your computer-based messages—are copied to your iPad, where you can now check for mail.

To set up mail accounts on your iPad:

1. Tap Settings > Mail, Contacts, Calendars > Add Account Ⓐ.

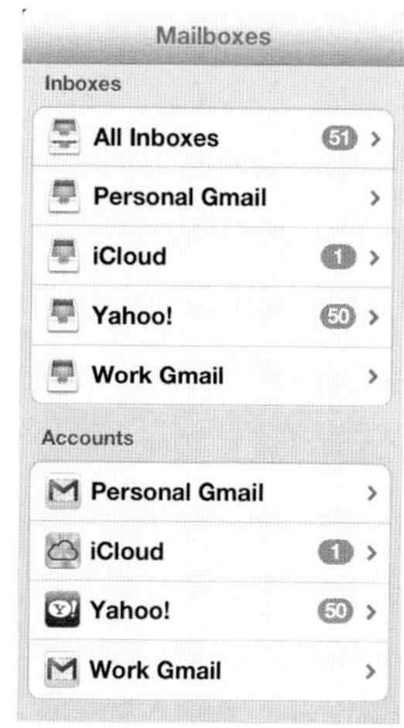

B The Mailboxes screen in Mail shows your inboxes and accounts. If this screen isn't visible, flick left to right.

2. Tap the icon for your mail provider, or tap Other if your provider isn't listed.
3. Type your name, email address, password, and a brief description (*Personal Gmail,* for example).

   If you tapped Other, see the Other Mail Accounts sidebar.
4. When you're done, tap Save.
5. Repeat steps 1–4 if you have more than one account.
6. Open Mail to retrieve your messages **B**.

   If you have more than one account, Mail shows a *unified inbox,* where you can see all your new messages for every account by tapping All Inboxes. You can still tap each inbox individually or tap an account name to see other mailboxes (Sent, Trash, Drafts, and so on).

TIP To delete an unwanted account, tap Settings > Mail, Contacts, Calendars; tap the name of the target account in the Accounts section; and then tap Delete Account.

Other Mail Accounts

If you don't see your mail provider listed in the Add Account screen **A**, tap Other > Add Mail Account to set up a POP or IMAP mail account manually. Use the account settings provided by your ISP (Internet service provider), account administrator, or employer. These settings include your email address, your password, and the addresses of your provider's incoming and outgoing mail servers (which look like *mail.servername.com* and *smtp.servername.com,* respectively).

POP (Post Office Protocol) accounts use an older messaging protocol that wasn't designed to check mail from multiple computers. Unless your provider saves copies of your mail on its server, a POP server transfers incoming mail to your computer (or iPad) before you read it. You won't get copies of messages when you log in from another computer because you've already downloaded them.

IMAP (Internet Message Access Protocol) servers keep all your mail online, letting you get the same mail on any computer or iPad you use. IMAP servers track which messages you've read and sent. If you run out of mailbox space on the IMAP server, you must delete old messages to prevent any new incoming mail from bouncing back to the senders. Most popular Web-based providers (Gmail, Yahoo, and so on) and modern organizations use IMAP.

Using Mail

Mail shows your mailboxes and accounts in a vertical list. Each message in the list shows the sender's name, a time stamp, the email's subject, and a two-line preview of the message.

In landscape (wide) view **A**, the list appears automatically. In portrait (tall) view, flick right or left to show or hide the list. Tap the list items to navigate among your mailboxes. To return to the previous mailbox, tap the arrow button in the top-left corner of the list.

TIP In portrait view, ▲ and ▼ also appear at the top of the screen; tap these icons to view the previous or next message.

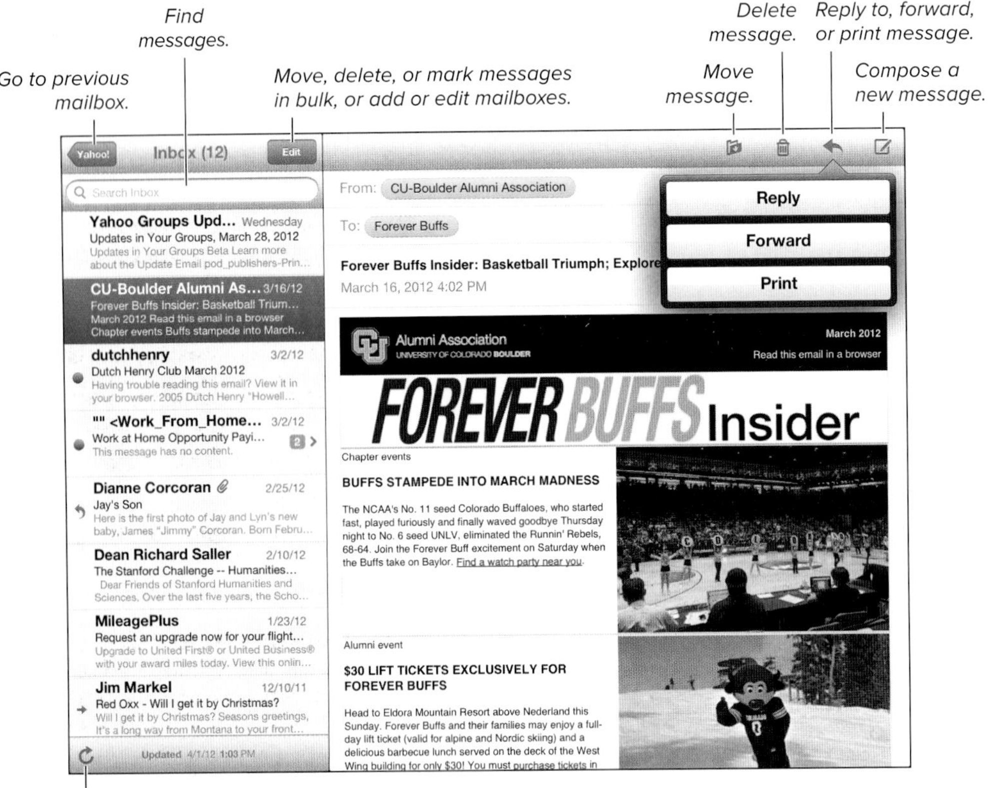

A Mail controls.

Here are some tips for using the mailbox list:

- Flick up or down to scroll the list.
- To find mail containing specific keywords, tap the Search field. You can search the To, From, and Subject fields and the body text of messages. Mail searches the downloaded messages in the current mailbox.

TIP You can also search for Mail messages from the Home screen. See "Searching Your iPad" in Chapter 2.

- A ● next to a message means you haven't read it. A ↩ means you've sent a reply. A ➡ means you've forwarded it.
- A numbered gray icon 3 > on the right side of a message preview refers to the number of messages in that *thread*—a set of messages grouped because they all have the same Subject line.
- Tap a message in the list to open it, complete with headers (From, To, Subject, and more), text, and attachments.
- Flick a message title in the list to delete it.

TIP Some providers, notably Gmail, turn the Delete button into an Archive button. A "deleted" message is actually moved to All Mail instead of Trash. If you prefer to delete to the trash, tap Settings > Mail, Contacts, Calendars; tap your account; and then turn off Archive Messages.

Reading Mail

You can read mail, open attachments, and use certain information in messages with other apps.

To read mail:

1. Open Mail.

   If you're connected to the Internet, Mail checks all your email accounts and downloads any new messages.

2. In the Mailboxes list, navigate to the desired mailbox and then tap a message preview.

   The message fills the screen (or most of it, in horizontal view **A**).

3. Read the message.

   If the message is long, flick to scroll it. To zip to the top of the message, tap the status bar at the top of the screen. Double-tap or pinch to zoom text and images.

4. When you're done reading the message, you can open another one by tapping it in the list or by tapping the ▲ and ▼ buttons.

TIP To mark multiple messages at the same time, tap Edit in the Mailboxes list, tap the target messages to select them, and then tap Mark at the bottom of the list.

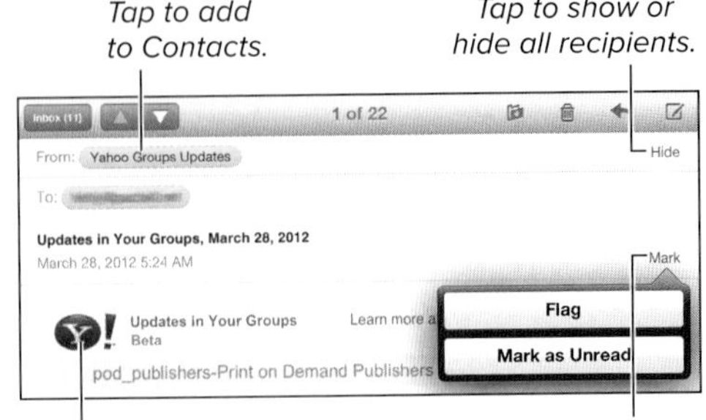

A Message controls.

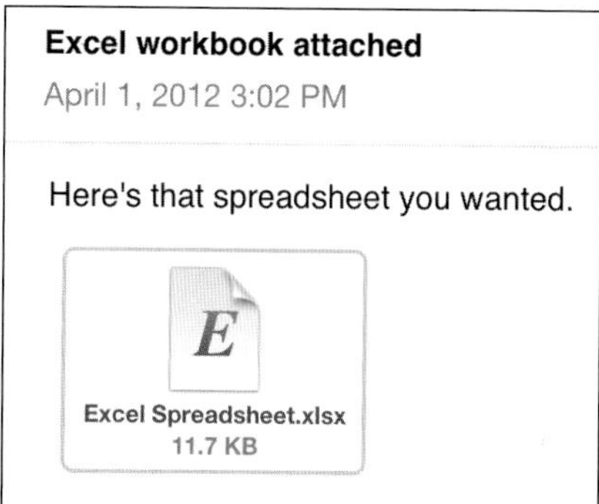

B Tap an attachment's icon to open it in the iPad's Quick Look previewer. In Quick Look, you can tap [icon] to open the attachment in a compatible app or print it.

C Touch and hold a blue link in a message to see a pop-up menu of options.

Viewing attached files

If an email message comes with files attached, Mail can display them. Mail supports

- Common photo and graphics formats (JPEG, PNG, GIF, and TIFF)
- Some audio formats (MP3, AAC, WAV, and AIFF)
- Some video formats (M4V, MP4, and MOV)
- PDF, RTF (Rich Text Format), and plain-text (.txt) files
- Web pages (.html and .htm files)
- vCard (.vcf) files, which you can add to Contacts (see Chapter 8)
- Microsoft Office files (Word, Excel, and PowerPoint)
- Apple iWork files (Pages, Numbers, and Keynote)

Photo attachments usually appear open and visible in the message. Other attachments typically appear as icons at the bottom of the message **B**. Tap an attachment's icon to preview it.

Using links and detected data

Mail recognizes dates, phone numbers, postal addresses, Web addresses, and certain other types of information in messages. If you see a bit of text underlined in blue, touch and hold that link to open a pop-up menu **C**. Depending on the type of information the link represents, you can display a location in Maps, add info to Contacts, create an event in Calendar, open a Web page in Safari, copy text to the Clipboard, and more. Mail even recognizes phrases like *dinner tomorrow*.

Writing and Sending Mail

You can use Mail to send a message to anyone who has an email address.

TIP To set whether an alert sounds when you send or receive mail, tap Settings > General > Sounds.

To write and send a message:

1. To start from scratch, tap at the top of the screen.

   or

   To reply to (or forward) a message, tap at the top of the screen and then tap Reply, Reply All, or Forward.

   Either way, Mail creates a new message **A**.

TIP If you reply, files or photos attached to the original message aren't sent back. To include attachments, forward instead of reply.

2. To add a recipient, tap the To field at the top of the message and then type the recipient's email address.

   If the recipient is in your Contacts list or if you've written to the person before, Mail autosuggests addresses as you type (which you can tap or ignore).

   or

   Tap to pop open your Contacts list and then tap the recipient's name.

TIP To delete a recipient, tap the recipient's name and then tap on the keyboard.

3. If you want to send copies of the message to other people, tap the Cc (carbon copy) or Bcc (blind carbon copy)

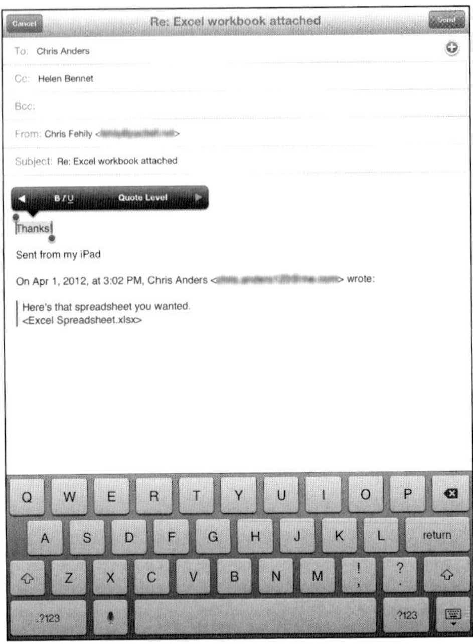

A You can add message recipients from your Contacts list or type their email addresses manually.

field and then fill it out as you did the To field.

or

Drag addresses between the fields.

TIP **Bcc recipients aren't disclosed to the message's other recipients. It's common to use Bcc when you're addressing many recipients or recipients who don't necessarily know one another (members of a mailing list, for example).**

4. If you have multiple mail accounts, tap the From field and then choose the account you want to send from.
5. Tap the Subject line and then type whatever this message is about.

   If you're replying to or forwarding a message, you can edit the existing subject.
6. Tap the message body area and then type your main text.

TIP **For tips on typing on the onscreen keyboard, see Chapter 2.**

7. Format the message, if you want.

   To add character formatting, select the text in question; tap ▶ in the pop-up menu; and then tap BIU to apply the bold, italic, or underline style. To increase or decrease the indentation (if you're quoting a section from a previous message), tap Quote Level.
8. When you're done, tap Send in the top-right corner of the message, or tap Cancel to delete the message or save it as a draft for later.

TIP **To send a photo or video, open Photos or Videos, select the photo(s) or video(s), and then tap or Share. You can also copy and paste photos and videos into a message. To send contact information, open Contacts, select a contact, and then tap Share Contact in the contact's Info screen.**

Changing Mail Settings

Mail comes with standard settings for the text size, default account, and more. If you don't like what you see, tap Settings > Mail, Contacts, Calendars and then change any of the following settings in the Mail section **A**:

Show. Set the number of recent messages to show in a mailbox. To download additional messages, scroll to the bottom of the mailbox list and then tap the link.

Preview. Show more or fewer preview lines for each message in the list. These lines let you scan a list of messages in a mailbox and get an idea of what each message is about.

Minimum Font Size. Make message text larger or smaller for more comfortable reading.

Show To/Cc Label. Choose whether To and Cc labels appear in the preview list.

Ask Before Deleting. Choose whether you must confirm that you want to delete a message.

Load Remote Images. Choose whether *remote images*—images located on a server rather than embedded in the message—are displayed in messages. Spammers and advertisers tend to use remote images to reduce their bandwidth costs and find out whether you open their messages.

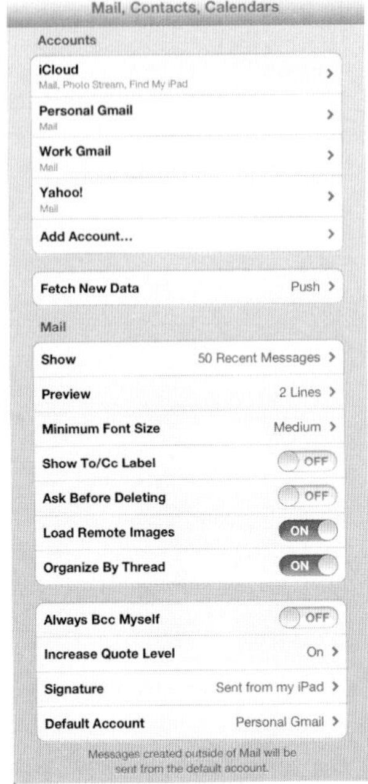

A You can change Mail's default settings here.

Organize By Thread. Choose whether messages with the same Subject line are grouped in the preview list. (Threaded messages are the ones with the 3 > icons.)

Always Bcc Myself. Choose whether you get a copy of every message you send.

Increase Quote Level. Choose whether Mail indents sections of the original message when you reply.

Signature. Add an optional personalized tag to the bottom of each outgoing message. Typically, a signature is your name, title, contact info, or—if you must—a favorite quote or legal disclaimer.

Default Account. If you have multiple mail accounts, designate one as the default when you send a message from another app. When you send a photo from Photos or tap the email address of a business in Maps, for example, the message is sent from the default account. Note that you can still tap the From field to switch to a different account on a case-by-case basis.

Maps

You can use Maps to find locations and businesses, mark spots on a map, find your current location, get directions, and show traffic conditions.

Maps needs an Internet connection (Wi-Fi or cellular signal) to download its cartographic and point-of-interest data, so don't rely on it for emergency directions or wilderness hikes.

Maps uses Location Services for many of its features. To enable Location Services, tap Settings > Location Services, turn on Location Services, and then turn on Maps. For details, see "Using Location Services" in Chapter 3. To disallow the use of Location Services by children and guests, tap Settings > General > Restrictions > Location.

In This Chapter

Finding a Location

You can search for bodies of water, geographic features, latitude–longitude coordinates, continents, countries, regions, provinces, states, cities, towns, neighborhoods, street addresses, postal or ZIP codes, roads, intersections, airports (names or three-letter codes), landmarks, parks, schools, businesses, and other points of interest. Partial words and misspellings sometimes work.

TIP To locate a lost or stolen iPad on a map, see "Securing Your iPad" in Chapter 1.

To find a location:

1. Tap the Search button at the top of the Maps screen.
2. To search for a local, nonspecific location, such as *coffee shop* or *movies,* scroll and zoom the map to narrow the area of interest, or tap ➤ to zoom to your current location.

TIP Flick or drag to scroll; pinch or double-tap to zoom.

Sample Searches

Maps can find a surprisingly wide range of locations. Experiment. Here are some sample searches:

5th & broadway	*strait of hormuz*	*disney world*
1 market st, san fran	*mariana trench*	*80309*
honolulu	*mt fuji*	*nw1 3hb*
pizza	*half dome*	*école polytechnique*
asia	*–22.9083, –43.2436*	*greenwich village*
apple store beijing	*big ben*	*lax*

Ⓐ If Maps drop multiple pushpins on the map, a bar appears over the best match. Tap ☰ in the Search or Address field to see a list of matches.

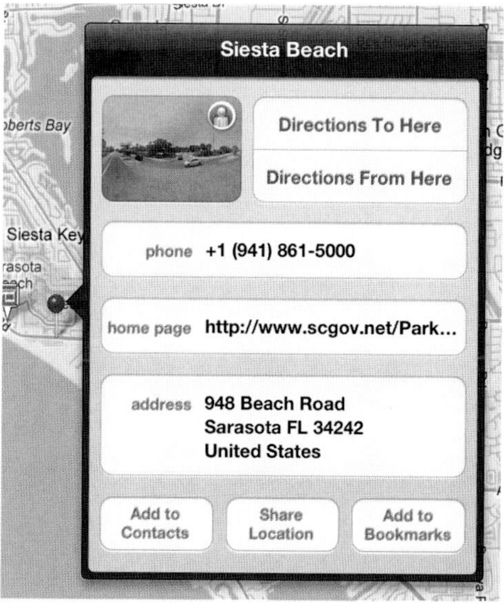

Ⓑ In the Info window, you can touch and hold textual information to copy it.

3. Tap the Search or Address field; type a location; tap Search on the keyboard; and if Maps opens a Did You Mean window, tap one of the listed locations.

   or

   Tap 📖 to find a previously bookmarked place, a recently found location, or a contact.

   Maps drops a pushpin on the map location or several pushpins on multiple matching locations Ⓐ.

4. To get more information about a location, tap its pushpin and then tap ⓘ Ⓑ.

   Use the Info window to show Street View (see the nearby sidebar), get directions, get the phone number, make a FaceTime call, visit the Web site, see the full address, add the location to Contacts, share (tweet, text, or email) the location, or bookmark the location. Available information varies by location.

continues on next page

5. To change the map view, tap or drag the bottom-right corner of the screen (the "page curl") and then tap a view **C**.

   You can also print your map from this screen. For details, see "Printing from Your iPad" in Chapter 2.

TIP To mark a specific spot on the map, touch and hold the spot to drop a pushpin on it. If you miss slightly, press and drag the pin to the right place. To drop a pin in the middle of the current map view, tap the bottom-right corner of the screen and then tap Drop Pin C. To remove a dropped pin, tap it, tap ⓘ, and then tap Remove Pin.

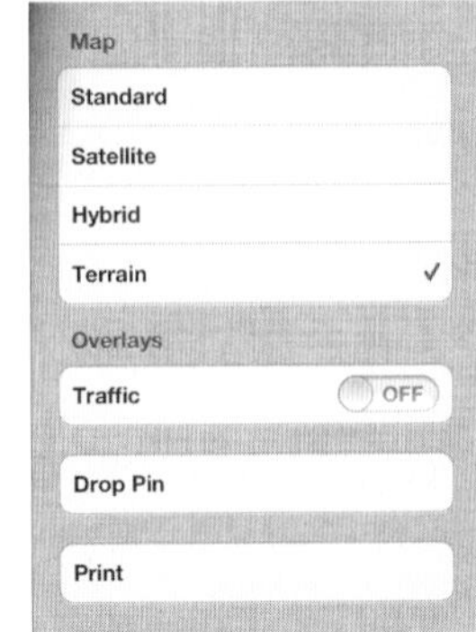

C The available map views are Standard (traditional cartography), Satellite (orbital photos), Hybrid (place and street names overlaid on satellite photos), and Terrain (shaded elevations).

Street View

Street View **D** shows ground-level photos merged into a 360-degree panoramic view. If this feature is available for a location, the Street View icon appears on the pushpin's pop-up bar **A** and Info window **B**.

In Street View, you can

- Flick or drag to pan the view.
- Pinch or double-tap to zoom.
- Tap the screen to show or hide the location and toolbar controls.
- Tap an arrow to move down a street.

The map inset in the bottom-right corner shows your current view. To return to map view, tap the inset or tap Done in the toolbar.

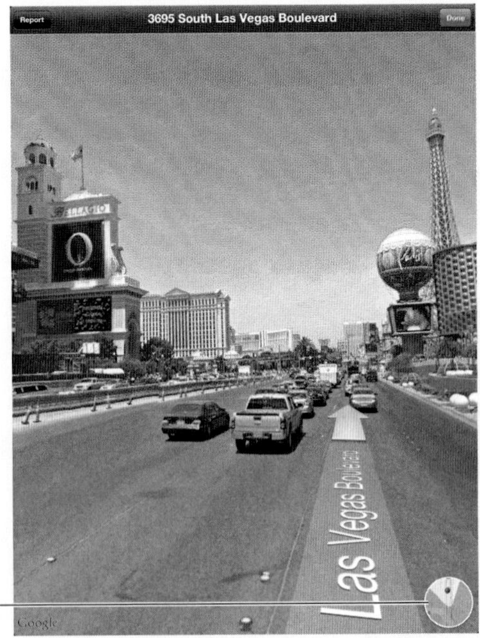

D Street View.

A Maps shows the approximate travel time for your trip.

Getting Directions

Maps can get you from Point A to Point B whether you're driving, walking, or taking public transportation.

To get directions:

1. Tap the Directions button at the top of the Maps screen.
2. In the Start and End fields, enter your origin and destination.

   Specify street addresses or locations as described in "To find a location" earlier in this chapter. You can tap to use your current location; use a dropped pin; or choose a location from your list of bookmarks, recent locations, or contacts.

   Maps calculates the route's step-by-step directions (including alternative routes, if available) and displays travel time for walking and driving routes in a blue toolbar at the bottom of the screen **A**.

TIP **The approximate travel time doesn't appear for public transit.**

3. To drive, tap ; to take public transit (bus, train, or ferry), tap ; or to walk, tap .

   Depending on the route, not every mode of transportation may be available. If you choose public transit, tap to schedule your trip.

continues on next page

4. To view directions one step at a time, tap Start and then tap ⬅ or ➡ to see the previous or next leg of the trip.

   or

   To view all the directions in a list, tap Start and then tap ▤ **B**.

5. If alternative routes appear on the map, you can tap the one that you want to use.

   The top item in the Directions list indicates your chosen route **B**. To view or choose another route, hide the Directions list. You may have to scroll or zoom the map to see the other routes, which are shown in light blue and labeled Route 1, Route 2, and so on.

6. To see current traffic conditions along the route (where available), tap the bottom-right corner of the screen and then turn on Traffic.

   Streets and highways are color-coded to indicate the flow of traffic: green = fast, yellow = slow, red = stop-and-go, and gray = no data.

TIP To use the digital compass, tap ➚ to find your current location and then tap ➚ again. The icon changes to ⚲, and a small compass appears ✵ onscreen, pointing north. Walk or turn around to get a heading. When you're done, tap ⚲.

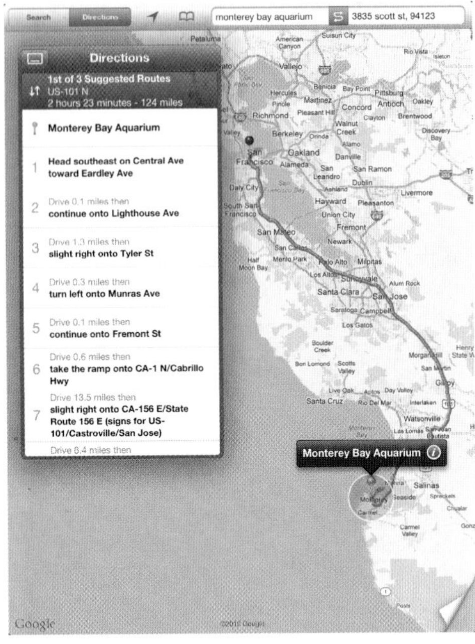

B Tap any item in the Directions list to see a map showing that leg of the trip. To hide the list, tap the button in the top-left corner.

15

Messages

Messages lets you send unlimited free text messages, photos, videos, and more to people who are also running Messages on their iPads, iPhones, iPod touches, or Macs, and with whom you've exchanged email addresses. Messages identifies you by your Apple ID email address and requires an Internet connection (Wi-Fi or cellular signal).

Messages uses Apple's *iMessage* instant-messenger service, a free alternative to the ubiquitous SMS and MMS messaging services used on mobile phones and the Web. iMessage works only on iDevices and Macs.

In This Chapter

Setting Up Messages

iMessages are displayed on all your iOS devices logged in to the same account. You can start a conversation on, say, your iPad and then continue it on your iPhone or iPod touch. Set up Messages on each device, using the same email address (or addresses).

TIP To use Messages, you and your recipients must be running iOS 5 or later.

To set up Messages:

1. Tap Settings > Messages.

   The iMessage screen opens **A**.

2. The first time you visit this screen, sign in with your Apple ID to activate the iMessage service.

   After you sign in, the Messages screen appears.

3. Turn on iMessage **B**.

   You can turn off this setting any time you don't want to be pestered.

4. To enable senders to get notifications when you've read their messages, turn on Send Read Receipts.

TIP If you want to be notified when your sent messages are read, recipients must turn on this setting on *their* devices. To toggle notifications, tap Settings > Notifications > Messages.

5. To add additional email addresses to your iMessage account, tap Receive At and then type more addresses.

   You can use any of your email addresses (work or home, for example).

6. If you want to add an email-style Subject line to your messages (typically, you don't), turn on Show Subject Field.

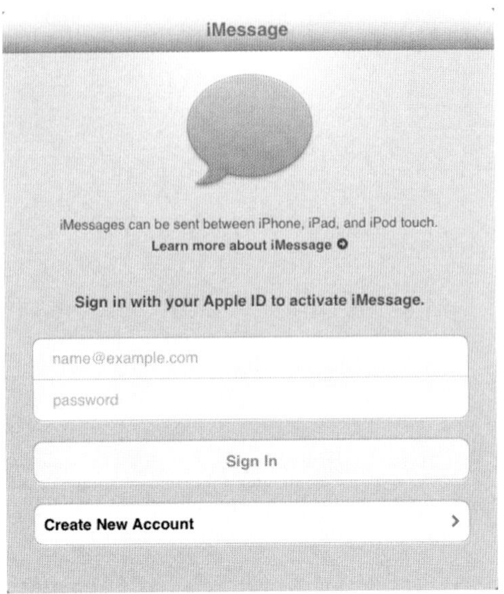

A You can create a new account if you don't already have one or if you don't want to use your existing account for messaging.

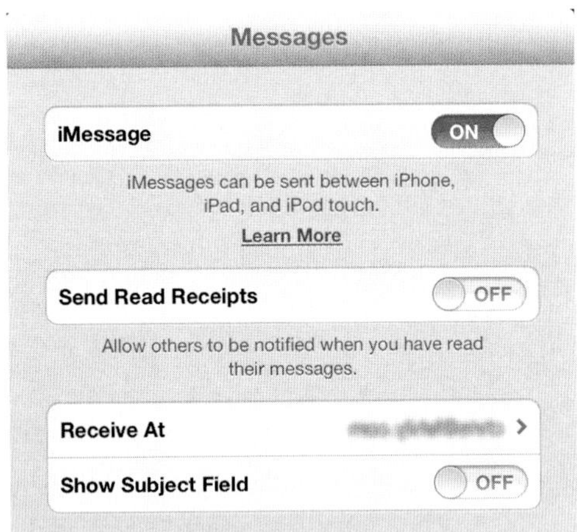

B Everyone with whom you want to chat must also turn on iMessage on their devices.

Having a Conversation

You can carry on multiple conversations at the same time and switch among them easily. Messages saves your conversations and lists them chronologically in the Messages list. You can resume, delete, edit, or forward your conversations at any time **A**.

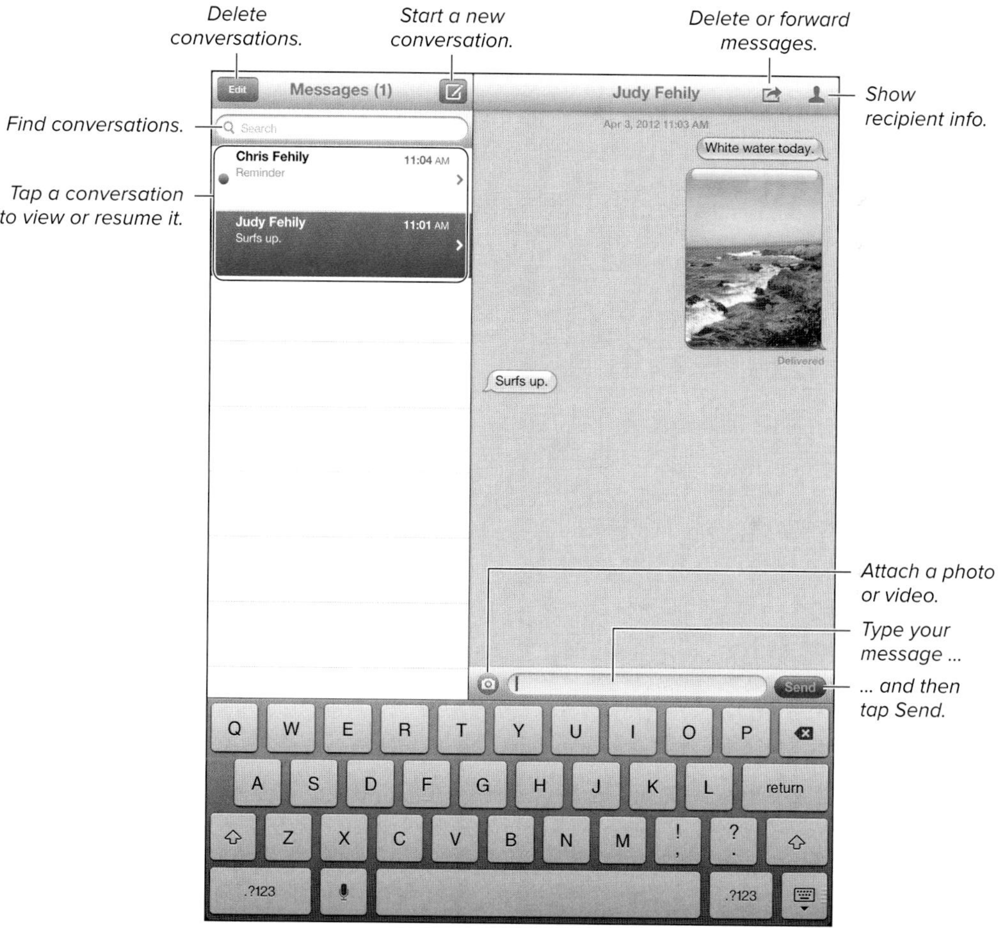

A Messages controls.

To start a conversation:

1. Tap .
2. Tap to choose a contact or type an email address manually.

   You can add multiple recipients (group chat). If Messages doesn't recognize someone, it displays .

TIP To delete a recipient, tap the recipient's name and then tap on the keyboard.

3. Tap the text field and then type your message.

   An ellipsis bubble (...) appears on the other person's screen, indicating that you're typing.
4. To attach a photo or video, tap .

   To save space, Messages may compress photo and video attachments.
5. Tap Send.

   If someone replies, you're having a conversation. For security, all iMessages are encrypted.

TIP An alert appears next to a message that can't be sent. Check your recipients list and then tap the alert to try to resend the message.

Messaging Tips

Here are some tips for using Messages:

- A in the Messages list indicates an unread message.
- You can flick a conversation in the Messages list to delete it.
- Touch and hold a message bubble to copy its contents. Tap a photo or video bubble to view, play, or save it.
- For general typing and editing tips, see Chapter 2.
- To type smiley faces and other picture characters, add the Emoji keyboard. See "Using International Keyboards" in Chapter 2.
- You can search for messages from the Home screen. See "Searching Your iPad" in Chapter 2.
- To set whether an alert sounds for incoming messages, tap Settings > General > Sounds.
- To send a location from Maps (see Chapter 14), tap for a location, tap Share Location, and then tap Message. To send contact info from Contacts (see Chapter 8), choose a contact, tap Share Contact, and then tap Message.

16

Newsstand

Newsstand gathers all your magazine and newspaper app subscriptions in a central place. Newsstand itself isn't an app: It's actually a special folder that's created and maintained by your iPad. You can't delete Newsstand or drag it into another folder.

In This Chapter

Using Newsstand

Each publication in Newsstand is a standalone app, which you can download from the App Store the way you do any other app. The quickest way to get to the store is to tap Newsstand and then tap the Store button **A**. Alternatively, open App Store, tap Top Charts or Categories (at the bottom of the screen), and then choose the Newsstand category.

Tapping a publication's app opens its own home screen, showing past and current issues **B**. You can buy an autorenewable subscription or buy single issues as individual in-app purchases. Purchases are billed to your Apple ID account.

TIP To get help for a publication, see the app's built-in help or its Info screen in App Store.

A Newsstand opens to reveal your magazine and newspaper apps.

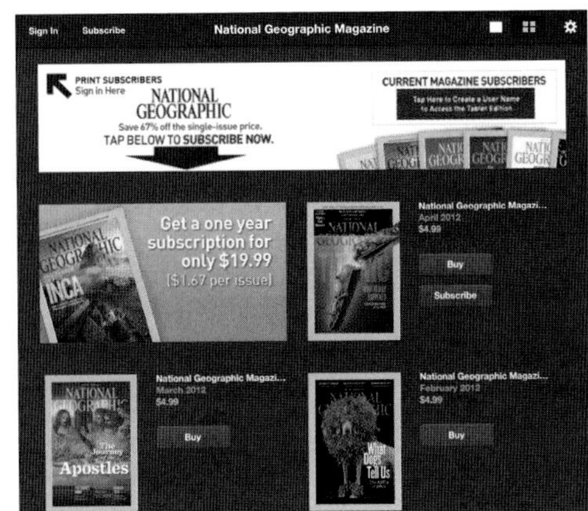

B Apple doesn't enforce a consistent style, so each publication has its own design and navigational controls.

Managing Newsstand

Newsstand-compatible apps move into Newsstand automatically. You can't drag other publications (or books) into Newsstand. If a subscription app or publication doesn't appear in Newsstand, the publisher hasn't enabled that app for Newsstand.

An alert badge, in the form of a small number in a red circle, appears on the Newsstand icon when new issues arrive. Newsstand updates subscriptions (downloads new issues) over only Wi-Fi—not cellular connections.

To turn on automatic downloads for your publications:

- Tap Settings > Store.

TIP Some publication apps have additional settings; look in the left column of the Settings screen.

To rearrange Newsstand apps:

1. Touch and hold any app icon for a few seconds until all the icons wiggle.
2. Drag icons to new locations within Newsstand.
3. Press the Home button.

To delete a Newsstand app:

- Tap ⊗ on the app's icon while all the icons are wiggling.

Notes

Notes lets you type notes on a virtual pad of scratch paper. It's also a handy place to paste text copied from Safari, Mail, Maps, and other apps. (You can't paste photos or media into Notes.)

In This Chapter

Reading and Writing Notes

You can rotate your iPad to read and write notes in portrait or landscape orientation. In portrait view, tap Notes in the top-left corner to open a list of your notes. In landscape view, the list of notes appears on the left, and the current note is circled Ⓐ.

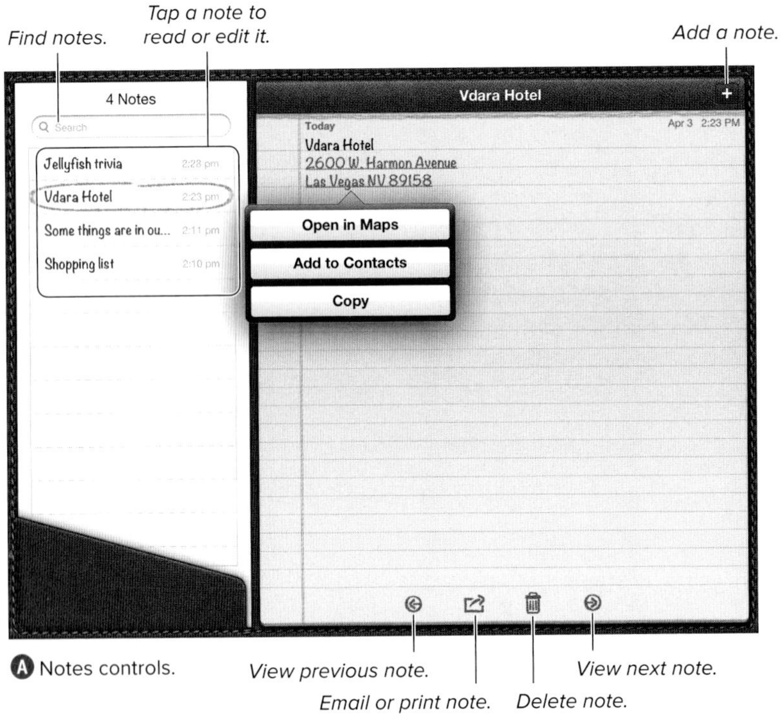

Ⓐ Notes controls.

Notes Tips

Here are some tips for using Notes:

- To change the font, tap Settings > Notes.
- To undo or redo your last edit, shake the iPad front to back to bring up an Undo/Redo box.
- You can flick a note in the Notes list to delete it.
- To sync notes wirelessly across your devices, tap Settings > iCloud > Notes > On. For details, see "Using iCloud" in Chapter 4.
- You can search for notes from the Home screen. See "Searching Your iPad" in Chapter 2.

Notes are listed chronologically, with the most recently modified note at the top. Each item in the list shows the first few words of the note.

TIP For general typing and editing tips, see Chapter 2.

Notes recognizes dates, phone numbers, postal addresses, Web addresses, and certain other types of information in messages. If you see a bit of underlined text, touch and hold that link to open a pop-up menu A. Depending on the type of information the link represents, you can display a location in Maps, add info to Contacts, create an event in Calendar, open a Web page in Safari, copy text to the Clipboard, and more. Notes even recognizes phrases like *lunch today*.

18

Photo Booth

On an iPad 2 or later, you can use Photo Booth to take a photo and apply a special effect to the shot.

In This Chapter

Taking and Viewing Photos

Photo Booth works with the front camera (for head shots) or back camera. Special effects include funhouse-mirror distortions, a thermal-image simulation, and a fake x-ray filter. The photos you take with Photo Booth are saved in your Camera Roll album in the Photos app.

To take a photo:

1. Open Photo Booth.
2. Tap the effect you want to apply **A**.
3. If you selected a distortion effect, you can drag, flick, pinch, or rotate the image to change the distortion **B**.

   or

   To select a different effect, tap [effects icon].

   or

   To swap the front and back cameras, tap [camera swap icon].
4. Tap [camera button] to take the photo.

   A thumbnail image of the photo slides into view above the controls. Flick left or right to view more thumbnails.

A You can take a normal photo (center box) or select a special effect.

B You can use multitouch gestures to further distort the image.

To view a photo:

- To see a photo full-size, tap its thumbnail.

To delete a photo:

- Tap it and then tap ⊗.

To manage photos:

1. Tap .
2. Tap one or more thumbnails.
3. Tap Email, Copy, or Delete.

TIP If you don't see the controls, tap the screen to show them.

19

Photos

Photos is the central app for viewing and managing photos that you've taken with your iPad's camera (iPad 2 or later); imported from your digital camera; synced with your computer; or saved from email, text messages, or the Web. The iPad can display photos and graphics in most popular image formats, including JPEG, PNG, TIFF, GIF, and RAW. You can also use Photos to view and manage videos that you take with the built-in camera or import from a digital camera or other iDevice.

In This Chapter

Getting Photos onto Your iPad

You can get pictures onto your iPad in the following ways.

Built-in camera. Photos and videos taken with Camera (see Chapter 7), as well as photos taken with Photo Booth (see Chapter 18), appear automatically in Camera Roll. To view your Camera Roll album, tap Photos > Camera Roll.

TIP On an iPad 1, which has no built-in camera, Camera Roll is named Saved Photos.

Saved photos. To save a photo from an email, text message, or Web page, touch and hold the image and then tap Save Image in the pop-up menu. The photo is stored in Camera Roll. If an email has multiple photos attached to it, tap ↰ to save them all Ⓐ.

Screen shots. To capture an image of whatever is on your iPad's screen (like the figures in this book), press and release the Sleep/Wake button and the Home button at the same time. The shot lands in Camera Roll.

Photo Stream. You can use iCloud to automatically download to your iPad copies of photos synced from your computer or from another iDevice. Tap Settings > Photos > Photo Stream (or Settings > iCloud > Photo Stream). For details, see "Using iCloud" in Chapter 4.

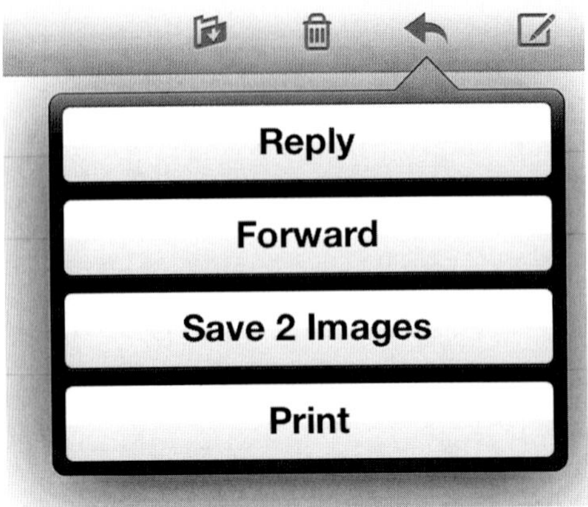

Ⓐ If an email has multiple images attached, Mail lets you save them all at the same time.

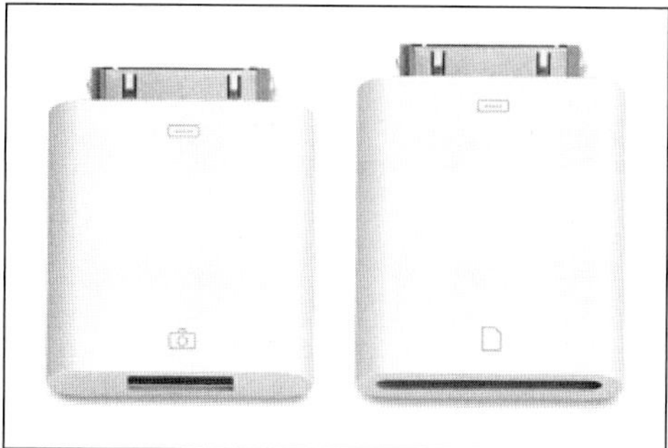

Ⓑ The Apple iPad Camera Connection Kit. You can use these adapters to suck photos into your iPad from an SD card or directly from your camera via USB cable.

Apple iPad Camera Connection Kit. This kit, available separately at http://store.apple.com, contains two adapters for the iPad's dock connector Ⓑ. One adapter is a port for your camera's USB cable, and the other has a slot for a Secure Digital (SD) memory card. After you plug in an adapter and insert a memory card or connect your camera, open Photos (if it doesn't open automatically). Tap Import All to get all the photos, or tap individual photos to select them before you tap Import. Photos then gives you the option to delete the photos on your camera or memory card after you import them. To see the imported photos, tap Photos > Last Import. You can sync the photos back to your computer by choosing the Import command in Adobe Photoshop Elements, iPhoto, or whatever photo-editing software you use.

iTunes sync. Connect your iPad to your computer via USB cable or Wi-Fi Sync, click your iPad in the iTunes sidebar (on the left side), click the Photos tab, and then set Sync Photos options. When you're done, click Apply or Sync. You can sync from a photo-organizer program like Photoshop Elements or iPhoto or from a folder such as My Pictures (Windows), Photos (Mac), or the folder of your choice. For details, see "Syncing with iTunes" in Chapter 4.

TIP You can sync only one computer's photo library to your iPad. If you sync photos from a second computer, iTunes erases all the photos from the first one.

Finding Photos on Your iPad

Photos organizes your photo collection into groups. Tap one of the buttons at the top of the screen to see your photos sorted in different views, including these.

Photos. Tapping Photos displays thumbnails of all your pictures in one place, including photos that you didn't group into albums before you imported them Ⓐ. To share, copy, or delete selected photos or to add them to an album, tap .

Photo Stream. Tapping Photo Stream displays photos that iCloud automatically sent to your iPad over the Internet (see "Using iCloud" in Chapter 4). To share, copy, or delete selected photos, or to save them to an album before they're rotated out by new photos, tap .

Albums. Tapping Albums displays the Camera Roll album and synced photos grouped under the same album names as in your photo program (iPhoto, Photoshop Elements, or whatever) Ⓑ. You can also create albums directly in Albums view; see the next section for details.

Other views. If you sync your photos from iPhoto '09 or later on the Mac, you may see more buttons at the top of the screen, including Events (time-stamp groupings), Faces (facial-recognition groupings), and Places (geolocation groupings). Places also shows geotagged photos taken with a GPS-enabled camera.

Ⓐ Photos view works best if you don't have a huge number of photos on your iPad.

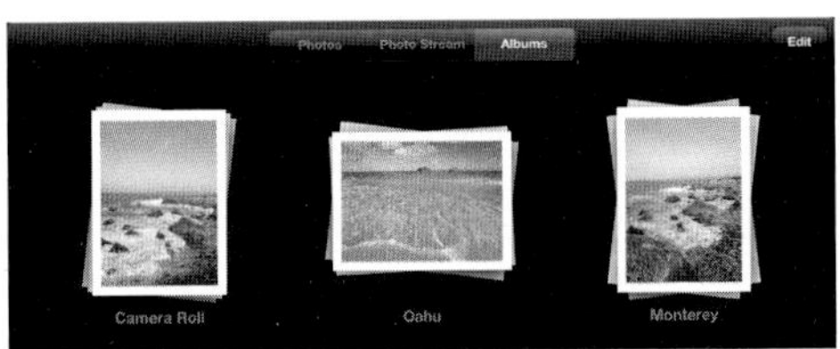

Ⓑ In Albums view, your picture sets look like stacks of loose photographs.

Ⓐ Spread your fingers slowly to view a clump of an album's photos without fully opening the album.

Working with Albums

Here are some tips for working with albums:

- To rearrange albums, touch and hold an album and then drag it.
- To see thumbnail images of all the photos in an album, tap the album.
- To see a quick preview of an album's photos, spread and then pinch your fingers on the album Ⓐ.
- To create an album, tap Edit > New Album, type an album name, and then tap Save. On the screen of photos that appears, tap to select the photos that you want to add to the new album and then tap Done.

TIP Albums created on your iPad aren't synced back to your computer.

- To rename an album, tap Edit and then tap the album name.
- To close an album, tap Albums or pinch the screen.
- To delete an album (but not its photos), tap Edit and then tap ⊗ on the album.
- To remove photos from an album (but not delete the photos), tap the album, tap ↗, tap to select the photos, and then tap Remove.
- To add photos from Photos view to a new or existing album, tap the Photos button, tap ↗, tap to select the photos, and then tap Add To.

TIP Some of these tips don't apply to albums synced from your computer. To manage synced albums, connect your iPad to your computer, open iTunes, click your iPad in the iTunes sidebar, and then click the Photos tab.

Viewing Photos

To view a photo (or video), tap one of the buttons at the top of the screen (Photos or Albums, for example) and then tap or spread an image's thumbnail to view it full-screen Ⓐ. Rotate your iPad to make a horizontal or vertical photo fill the screen's width or height.

You can do any of the following things:

- To show or hide the controls, tap the screen.
- To scroll through photos, flick left or right.
- To zoom a photo, double-tap, pinch, or spread.
- To pan a zoomed photo, drag or flick.
- To play a video, tap ▶.
- To edit a photo or trim a video, tap Edit. (For details, see "Using Photo and Video Tools" in Chapter 7.)
- Tap [share icon] to email a photo, assign it to one of your contacts, set it as wallpaper, tweet it to followers, print it, or copy it.

TIP A quicker way to copy a photo: Touch and hold the photo and then tap Copy in the pop-up menu. You can paste a copied photo (or video) into an email or text message.

- To delete a photo, tap [trash icon]. To delete photos from synced albums, connect your iPad to your computer, open iTunes, click your iPad in the iTunes sidebar, and then click the Photos tab.

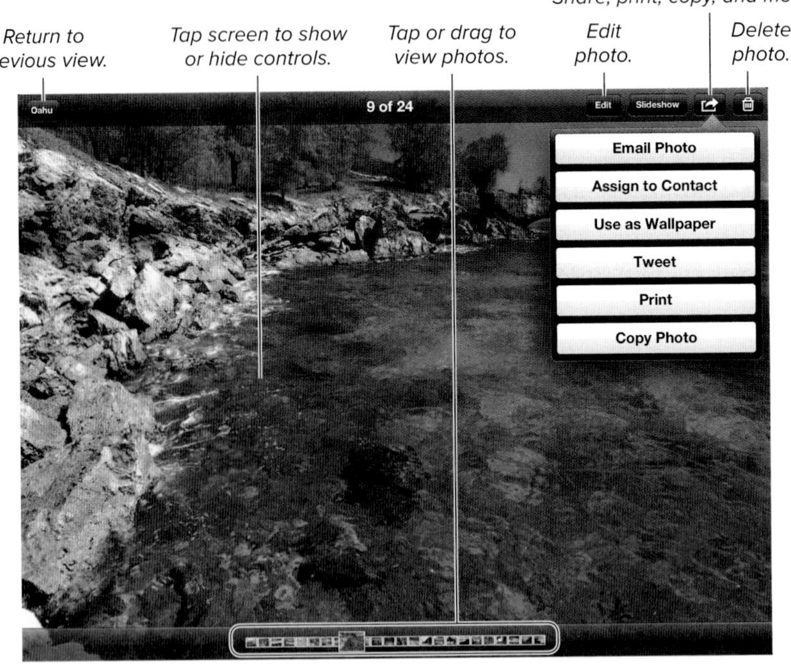

Ⓐ A full-screen photo, with controls showing.

Viewing a slideshow

A photo slideshow scrolls your photos automatically, with no need for you to tap and drag.

To set the timing and order of slides:

- Tap Settings > Photos.

To run a slideshow:

1. Switch to the Photos app.
2. Open an album, or go to Photos or Photo Stream view.
3. Tap the Slideshow button.
4. Select the transition and music options.
5. Tap Start Slideshow.

To stop a slideshow:

- Tap the screen.

TIP You can also stream a slideshow or video to a high-definition TV set (HDTV) via AirPlay. To do so, tap [AirPlay icon], if it appears. For details, see "Streaming with AirPlay" and "Screen Mirroring" in Chapter 3.

Displaying photos with Picture Frame

The iPad resembles a digital picture frame, and indeed, you can turn it into one by making the Lock screen display your photo collection—typically, while you recharge your iPad from a power outlet. You can display a slideshow of all your photos or of selected albums.

To set up Picture Frame:

1. Tap Settings > Picture Frame.
2. Select transition, timing, and other options.

To start Picture Frame:

1. Press the Sleep/Wake button to lock your iPad.
2. Press Sleep/Wake again to display the Lock screen.
3. Tap ⚙.

TIP If ⚙ doesn't appear on the Lock screen, tap Settings > General > Passcode Lock > Picture Frame > On.

To pause Picture Frame:

- Tap the screen.

To stop Picture Frame:

1. Tap the screen.
2. Tap ⚙.

Reminders

Reminders lets you create and manage to-do lists. You can add reminders to custom lists, assign them to future due dates, and mark them as completed to hide them from view.

In This Chapter

Creating and Managing Reminders and Lists

You can manage your to-do lists and fine-tune reminders by using the Reminders controls Ⓐ. You can create multiple to-do lists to keep your work, personal, and other tasks separate. Reminders comes with two lists: Reminders for active reminders and Completed for finished tasks.

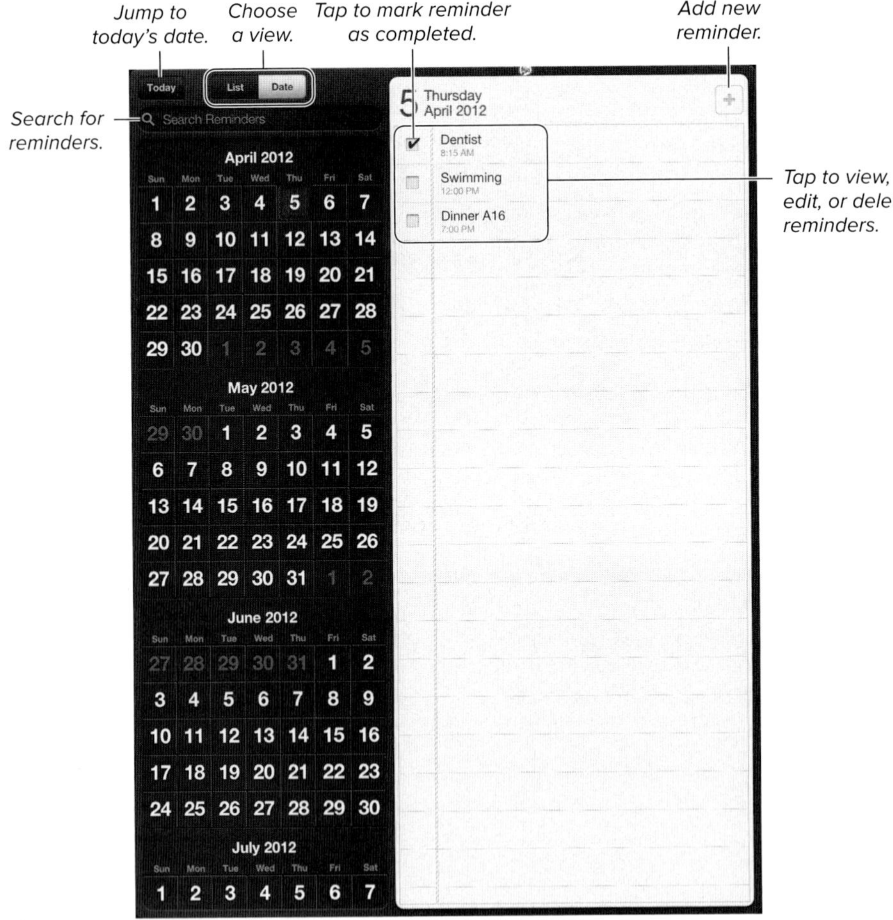

Ⓐ Reminders controls.

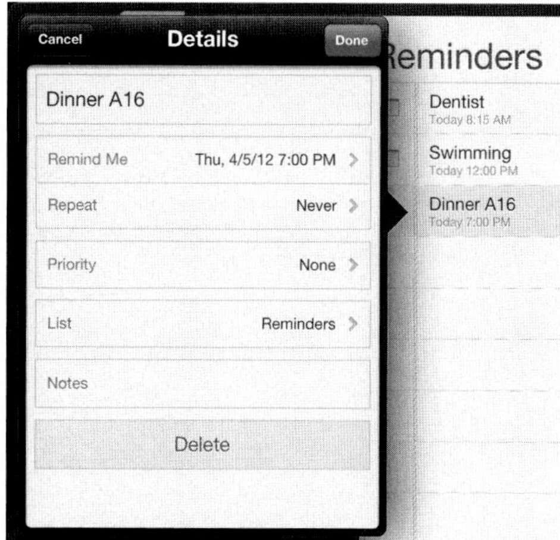

B You can edit or delete a reminder, set its date and time, add notes, move it to a different list, and more.

To add a reminder:

1. Tap **+** or tap the next empty item in the list.
2. Type a description for the reminder.
3. Tap Return.

To create a new list:

1. Tap List > Edit > Create New List.
2. Type a description for the list.
3. Tap Done.

TIP To set the default list for new reminders, tap Settings > Mail, Contacts, Calendars > Default List (below Reminders).

To manage your reminders and lists:

- To fine-tune a reminder, tap it **B**.
- To switch among lists, tap List and then tap a list name. In List view, you can also tap Edit to reorder, delete, or rename lists. (You can't edit or delete the Completed list, which shows reminders that you've marked as completed.)
- You can search for reminders from the Home screen. (See "Searching Your iPad" in Chapter 2.)
- To make reminders appear as notifications, tap Settings > Notifications > Reminders > Notifications Center > On. (For details, see "Getting Notifications" in Chapter 4.)
- To play audio alerts, tap Settings > General > Sounds > Reminder Alerts.

TIP If your iPad is turned off, a text alert appears when you turn it on, but audio doesn't play.

Syncing Reminders

When you have multiple devices, you can use iCloud to sync your reminders across them. Update your to-do lists in one place, and see your changes everywhere. For details, see "Using iCloud" in Chapter 4.

To sync your reminders across all your computers and iDevices:

- Tap Settings > iCloud > Reminders > On.

TIP On your computer, you can sync reminders with Outlook or with for iCal/Reminders for OS X.

To sync past reminders:

- Tap Settings > Mail, Contacts, Calendars > Sync (below Reminders).

TIP You can choose how far into the past to sync. Future reminders are always synced.

21

Safari

Safari is the iPad's Web browser. You can use it to download files and to display Web pages with text, graphics, animations, sounds, video, and links—but not Adobe Flash media, which isn't supported by iPad or other iDevices. Safari requires an Wi-Fi or cellular Internet connection.

Note that the Web is a *portion* of the Internet. (The terms are not synonyms.) The Internet contains not only the Web, but also channels for email (see Chapter 13), instant messages (see Chapter 15), and more.

In This Chapter

Browsing the Web

The important part of Safari is not the app itself, but the access it gives you to Web pages and other online resources. You'll spend most of your browsing time working within the Web itself—reading, searching, scrolling, zooming, tapping links, filling out forms, downloading files, and so on—rather than using Safari's controls Ⓐ.

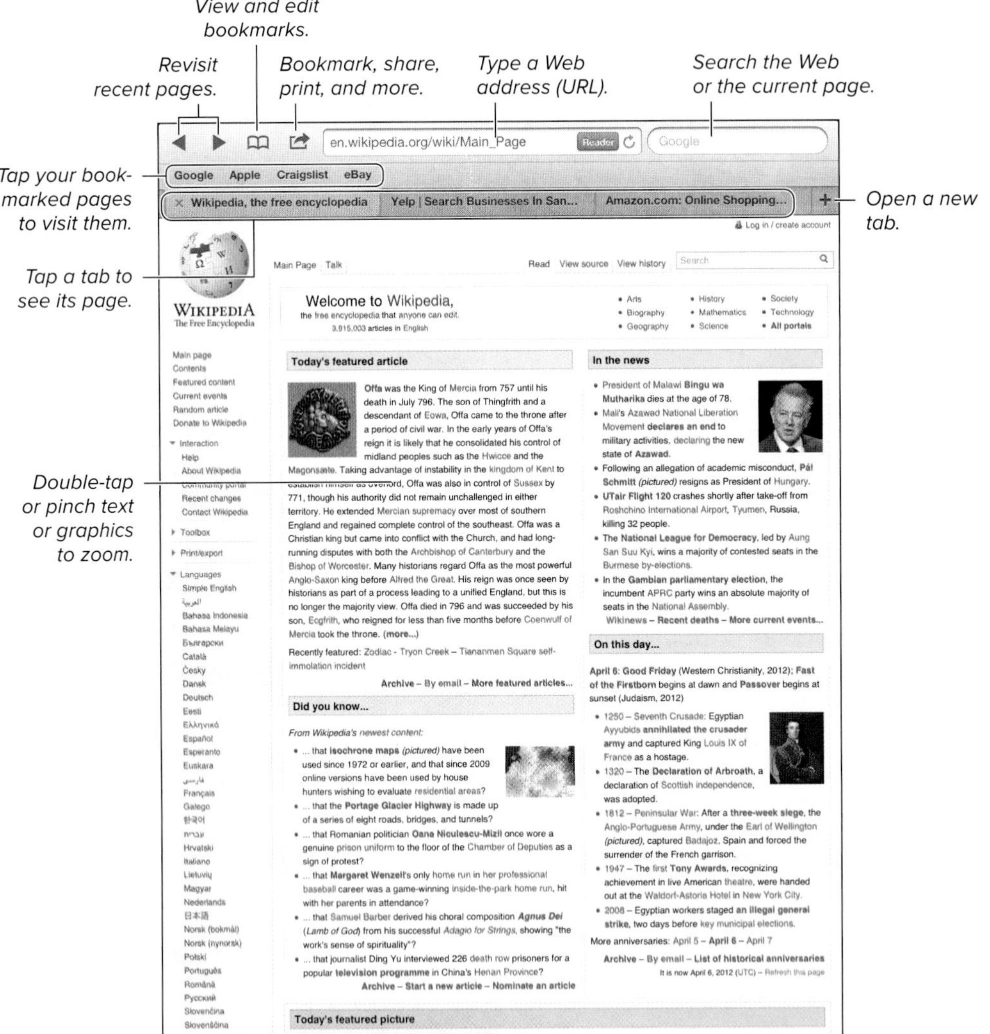

Ⓐ Safari and Web-site controls.

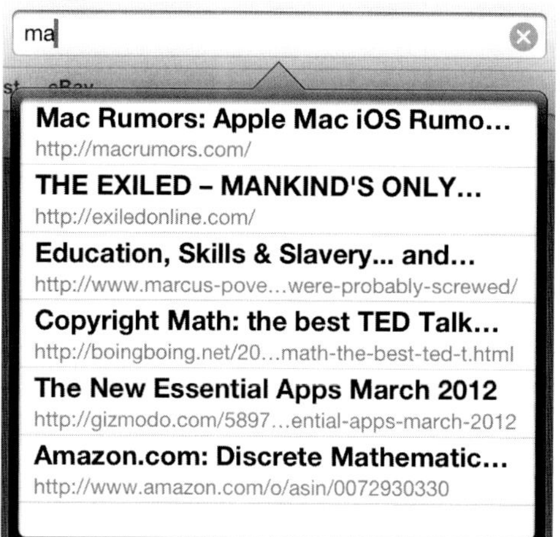

B As you type, Safari suggests matching addresses from your bookmarks and browsing history.

Like all modern browsers, Safari features tabbed browsing, which lets you open multiple Web pages on the same screen. You can open pages or links in new tabs and switch among them by tapping tabs. You can have up to nine tabs open at the same time.

To open a Web page:

1. Tap the Safari icon on the Home screen.

   The Safari screen appears, showing a blank page or the last page you had open during your previous browsing session.

2. To go to a specific Web page, tap the Address field, type or paste the address (URL), and then tap Go on the keyboard.

   or

   Tap one of the suggestions in the Address field's drop-down list **B**.

   Safari displays the Web page in the current tab.

TIP Press and hold the .com key to get your choice of .net, .org, .edu, and other top-level domains, depending on what country or region you've set your iPad for.

TIP To erase text in a field quickly, tap the field and then tap ⊗ in the field.

To search the Web:

1. Tap the Search field (labeled *Google* by default Ⓐ).
2. Type or paste search keywords and then tap Search on the keyboard.

   or

   Tap one of the suggestions (from the search engine) in the Search field's drop-down list.

   Safari displays the search provider's Web page, listing the search results ordered by relevance.

TIP To change the default search provider, tap Settings > Safari > Search Engine.

URLs

A *URL* (Uniform Resource Locator) is a case-insensitive address that identifies a Web page uniquely. The URL for Apple's home page, for example, is http://www.apple.com. The transmission standard for most Web pages is http://, so you don't type it; Safari fills it in for you. Secure (banking and commerce) Web sites use https://. The rest of the address specifies the Web server and the Web page's location on it. Some URLs don't need the www.; others require additional dot-separated elements.

The server name's last part, called the *top-level domain* (TLD), usually tells you about the Web site's owner or country. The domain .com is a business, .gov is a government, .edu is a school, .uk is a United Kingdom site, .ca is a Canadian site, and so on. For a list of TLDs, see www.iana.org/domains.

Web-page files are organized in folder trees on the server, so a long URL (www.apple.com/ipad/features/, for example) works like a path on a computer. Complicated URLs that contain ?, =, and & symbols are pages created on the fly in response to a query.

If a *Cannot Open Page* alert appears instead of a Web page, you may have mistyped the URL, or the Web page may have been moved or removed.

Navigating Web pages

You can do any of the following things when you navigate Web pages:

- **Scroll and zoom.** To scroll, flick or drag in any direction. To zoom in or out, double-tap, spread, or pinch. To scroll to the top of a page quickly (in most apps), tap the status bar at the top of the screen. To scroll within a frame (inset window) on a page, scroll with two fingers inside the frame.
- **Rotate your iPad.** You can view pages in either portrait (tall) or landscape (wide) view. Web pages scale automatically to the wider screen, making the text and images larger.
- **Reload the page.** To reload a stale or incomplete page, tap ↻ in the Address field Ⓐ.
- **Stop downloading a page.** If you request the wrong page or tire of waiting for a slow-loading page, tap ✕ in the Address field to stop the page from downloading any further.
- **Revisit pages.** To revisit pages that you've seen recently, tap or press and hold ◀ or ▶. To revisit pages that you've seen in the past week or so, tap 📖 > History.

TIP **To clear your browsing history, tap 📖 > History > Clear History.**

To view and manage tabs:

■ Do any of the following:
  - To view a different tab, tap it.
  - To open a new tab, tap ✚ on the tab bar.
  - To reorder tabs, drag them left or right on the tab bar.
  - To close a tab, tap the tab to activate it and then tap ✖ on the tab.

To search the current Web page:

1. Type or paste text in the Search field **A**.
2. Scroll to the bottom of the pop-up window and then tap the item below On This Page.
3. If multiple matches are found, tap ◀ or ▶ at the bottom of the screen to navigate among them.

To share the current page:

1. Tap [share icon] **C**.
2. Choose an action from the drop-down list:
   - Mail Link to This Page
   - Tweet
   - Print

TIP **For details on printing, see "Printing from Your iPad" in Chapter 2.**

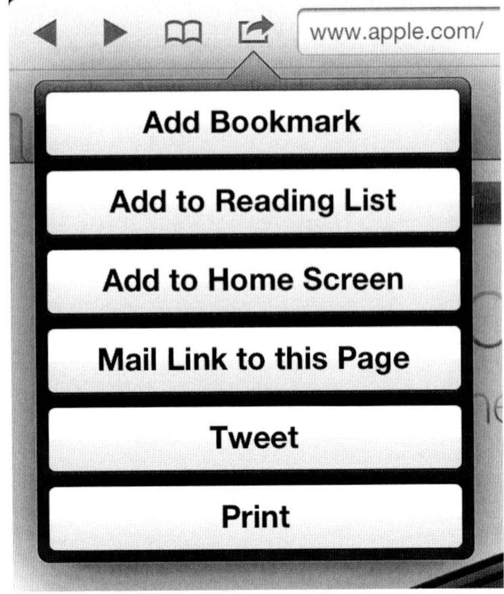

C You can email, print, or tweet the Web address of the current page.

Twitter

Twitter is a popular third-party micro-blogging service that you can access via several built-in apps. Tap Settings > Twitter to create a free account or sign in to your existing account.

You can send *tweets*—140-character messages—with attachments from multiple apps, including Safari, Camera, Photos, Maps, and YouTube. To tweet a photo, video, location, or Web page, tap [share icon] > Tweet.

While you're composing a tweet, the number in the bottom-right corner of the Tweet screen shows the number of characters remaining that you can enter (up to 140). Attachments use some of a tweet's characters.

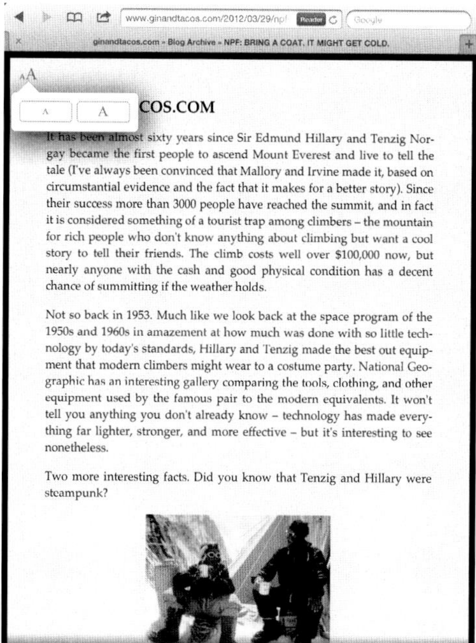

www.ginandtacos.com/2012/03/29/np Reader Google

ginandtacos.com » Blog Archive » NPF: BRING A COAT. IT MIGHT GET COLD.

AA

A A COS.COM

It has been almost sixty years since Sir Edmund Hillary and Tenzig Norgay became the first people to ascend Mount Everest and live to tell the tale (I've always been convinced that Mallory and Irvine made it, based on circumstantial evidence and the fact that it makes for a better story). Since their success more than 3000 people have reached the summit, and in fact it is considered something of a tourist trap among climbers – the mountain for rich people who don't know anything about climbing but want a cool story to tell their friends. The climb costs well over $100,000 now, but nearly anyone with the cash and good physical condition has a decent chance of summitting if the weather holds.

Not so back in 1953. Much like we look back at the space program of the 1950s and 1960s in amazement at how much was done with so little technology by today's standards, Hillary and Tenzig made the best out equipment that modern climbers might wear to a costume party. National Geographic has an interesting gallery comparing the tools, clothing, and other equipment used by the famous pair to the modern equivalents. It won't tell you anything you don't already know – technology has made everything far lighter, stronger, and more effective – but it's interesting to see nonetheless.

Two more interesting facts. Did you know that Tenzig and Hillary were steampunk?

D Reader strips a page of distracting junk.

Uncluttering pages

Safari's Reader feature strips pages of ads, graphics, toolbars, and other nonessential elements, letting you read without distractions. To view an article in Reader, tap Reader in the Address field (if it appears; not every page works with Reader) **D**. To adjust the font size, tap AA. To return to normal view, tap Reader again.

Bookmarking Web Pages

You can bookmark Web pages that you like and open them quickly in the future. As your bookmarks list grows, you can organize your bookmarks in folders.

To bookmark the current page:

- Tap [icon] > Add Bookmark.

To add a bookmark icon to the Home screen:

- Tap [icon] > Add to Home Screen.

To open a bookmarked page:

1. Tap [icon].
2. Tap the bookmark you want in the drop-down list **A**.

A Bookmarks are normally saved at the top level of the Bookmarks list.

Editing and reordering bookmarks

Bookmarks placed in the Bookmarks Bar folder appear on the bookmarks bar, above the tabs. To reach bookmarks placed in other folders, you must tap 📖. To edit, reorganize, or delete bookmarks, tap 📖 > Edit **A** and then drag or delete the bookmarks in the list.

TIP The bookmarks bar appears when you tap the Address field. To always show it, tap Settings > Safari > Always Show Bookmarks Bar.

Syncing bookmarks

To sync bookmarks wirelessly across your computers and iDevices, tap Settings > iCloud > Bookmarks > On. (For details, see "Using iCloud" in Chapter 4.)

You can also sync bookmarks with the browser on your computer. (See "Syncing with iTunes" in Chapter 4.)

Working with Links

Text links typically are colored phrases. Pictures and buttons can also be links.

Navigating links

To follow a link, tap it. To see a link's destination or open it in a new tab, touch and hold the link Ⓐ.

TIP To open new tabs behind the current tab, tap Settings > Safari > Open New Tabs in Background > On.

Ⓐ Touch and hold a link to see where it leads; open it in the current tab; open it in a new tab; add it to your reading list; or copy its URL to the Clipboard.

Saving links to read later

Safari's Reading List feature lets you quickly save links to Web pages that you want to read later. You can think of the reading list as being a special, temporary bookmarks list.

To add the current page to your reading list:

- Tap [share icon] > Add to Reading List Ⓐ.

To add a link to your reading list:

1. Touch and hold the link .
2. Tap Add to Reading List Ⓐ.

To view your reading list:

- Tap [bookmarks icon] > Reading List.

  Safari divides the list into two parts: All and Unread.

To remove an item from your reading list:

- Flick its entry and then tap Delete.

TIP If you use iCloud to sync your bookmarks, your reading list is synced too.

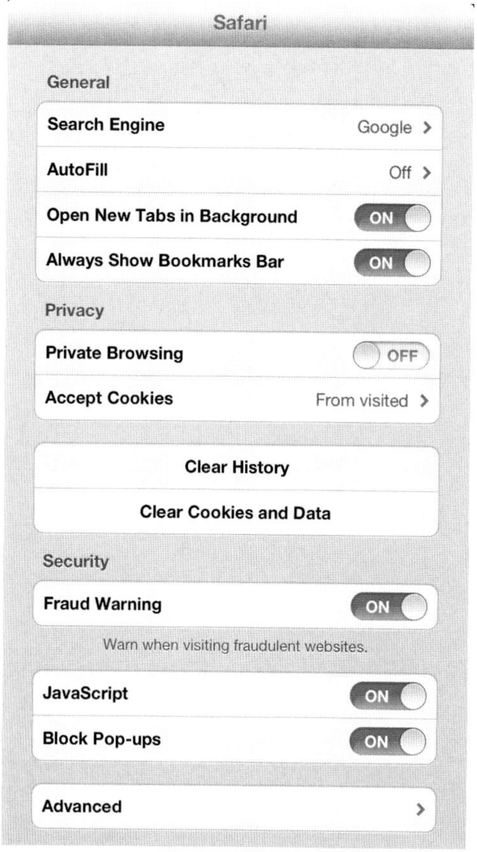

Ⓐ Set your privacy preferences here.

Managing Cookies, Privacy, and Security

Cookies are messages given to Safari by Web sites and stored on your iPad as small files. A cookie's main purpose is to identify you and possibly prepare customized Web pages for you. When you enter shopping preferences and personal information at, say, Amazon.com, that information is stored in a cookie, which Amazon can read when you return.

Most cookies are innocuous and spare you from having to fill out forms repeatedly, but some sites and advertisers use tracking cookies to record your browsing history.

To control cookies and privacy settings:

1. Tap Settings > Safari to open the Settings screen Ⓐ.
2. Configure the privacy and security settings the way you want them.

   To cover your tracks, clear your browsing history, cookies, and personal data. To hide from third-party advertisers, tap Accept Cookies > From Visited.

Autofilling Forms

Safari's AutoFill feature automatically fills in your name, address, and other contact info on Web forms, saving you from typing the same information repeatedly. (AutoFill is especially useful for frequent online shoppers.) The feature can also memorize your user names and passwords—convenient, but a potential disaster if you ever lose an iPad that isn't passcode-locked. (For details, see "Securing Your iPad in Chapter 1.)

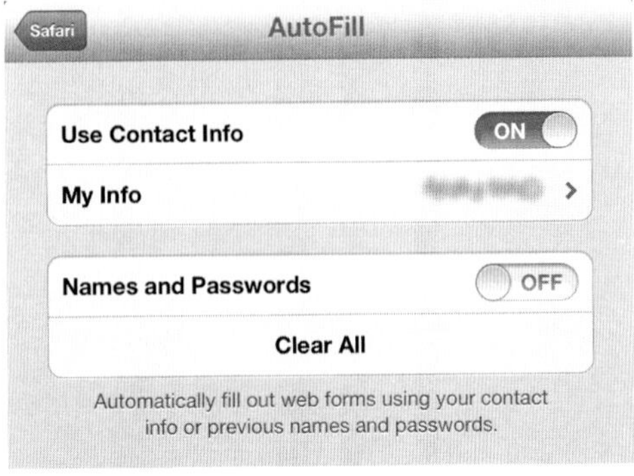

A Activate AutoFill here.

To use AutoFill:

1. Tap Settings > Safari > AutoFill **A**.
2. To make AutoFill enter your contact information on Web forms, turn on Use Contact Info.
3. To make AutoFill fill enter your user names and passwords on login screens, turn on Names and Passwords.

   AutoFill memorizes your login credentials the first time you enter them after turning on this setting.

TIP When AutoFill is turned on, you'll see an AutoFill button on the keyboard when you visit a Web form that wants your info. Tap it to enter the info.

Settings

Settings is the central screen for changing systemwide and app-specific settings on your iPad, similar to Preferences on the Mac or Control Panel in Windows. If you've used your iPad for even a little while, you've probably visited Settings.

In This Chapter

Viewing and Changing Settings

If you want to tweak the way your iPad or an app works, poke around in Settings to see what's available.

To view or change settings:

1. Tap the Settings icon on the Home screen.

   The Settings screen appears **A**.

2. Tap an item in the list on the left.

   This list identifies the services and apps that you can change, with headings such as Wi-Fi, General, and Safari. If an app that you downloaded from the App Store has additional settings, it appears at the bottom of the list, below Apps.

3. In the list on the right side, tap a label, link, or control to view or change a setting.

4. To backtrack to the previous screen, tap the arrow button at the top of the right list, or tap any item in the left list.

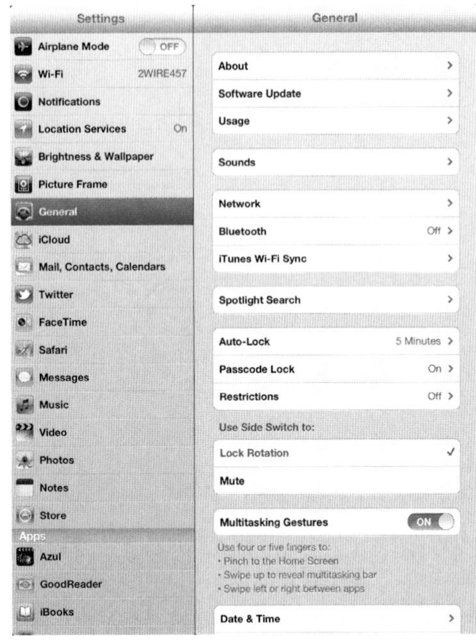

A The Settings screen.

23

YouTube

The YouTube app lets you watch videos submitted by people around the world. YouTube videos that you watch on the Web, at www.youtube.com, are often encoded in Adobe Flash format, which doesn't work on an iPad (or any other iOS device). The videos that you watch in the YouTube app are in H.264 format, which provides higher-quality rendering than Flash. YouTube requires an Internet connection.

In This Chapter

Watching Videos in the YouTube App

Millions of YouTube videos are available. You can watch them in full-screen view or with the video's Info page showing. The playback controls work about the same way that they do in other video apps.

To watch a YouTube video:

1. Tap the YouTube icon on the Home screen.
2. To browse for videos, tap one of the buttons at the bottom of the screen (Featured, Top Rated, and so on).

   or

   To search for videos, tap the YouTube field at the top of the screen, type a word or a phrase, and then tap Search.

TIP Some YouTube features require a YouTube account, which you can set up at for free at www.youtube.com.

3. Tap a video thumbnail to see that video's Info page **A**.

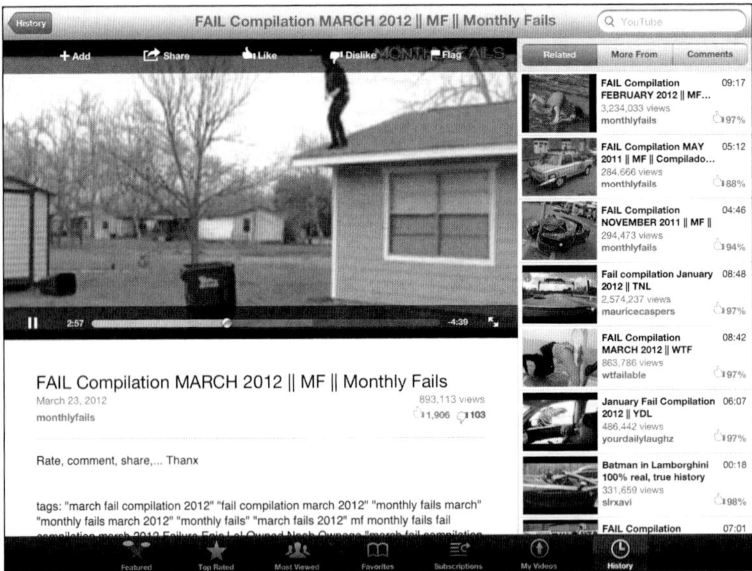

A A video's Info page shows a description, upload date, contributor, number of views, viewer ratings and comments, tags (keywords), clip length, links to related videos, and more.

4. If the video doesn't start playing automatically, tap ▶ to play it.

   After a few seconds, the playback controls **B** disappear so that they don't block the picture. Tap the video at any time to show or hide the controls.

TIP While watching in full-screen view, you can double-tap the video to toggle widescreen and full-screen display.

TIP To stream a video to a high-definition TV via AirPlay, tap [AirPlay icon], if it appears. For details, see "Streaming with AirPlay" in Chapter 3.

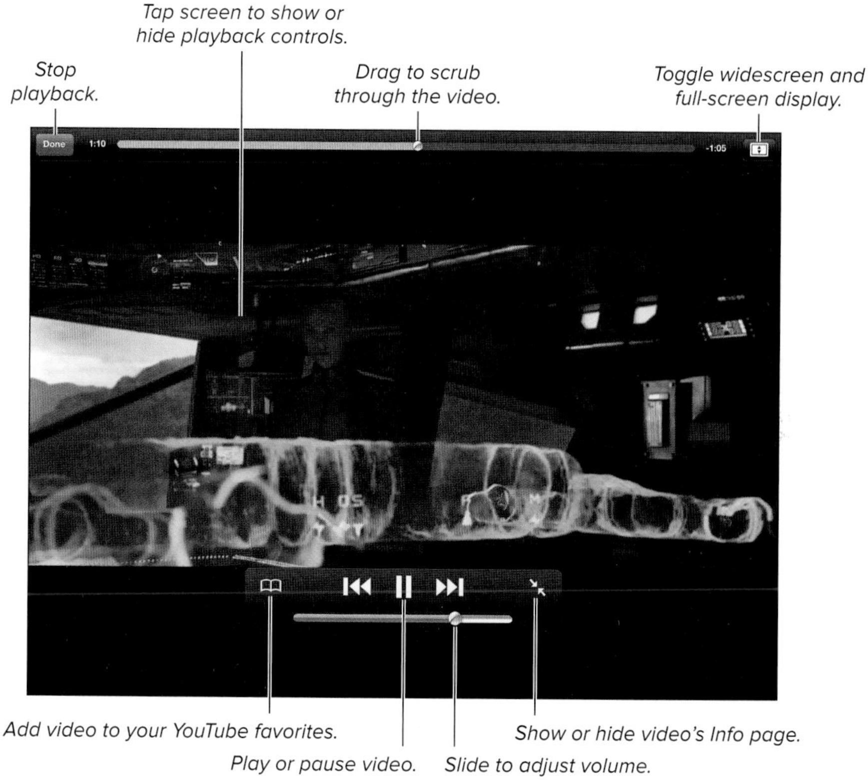

Tap screen to show or hide playback controls.

Stop playback.

Drag to scrub through the video.

Toggle widescreen and full-screen display.

Add video to your YouTube favorites.

Show or hide video's Info page.

Play or pause video.

Slide to adjust volume.

B YouTube playback controls for a full-screen video.

App Gallery

The App Store (see Chapter 5) has more than half a million apps, and even though Apple vets every one, plenty of junk gets through—mostly from small developers trying to cash in on the gold rush. In general, the app reviews posted by users aren't particularly trustworthy or useful; their quality usually is poor, and they provide no place for developers to respond to erroneous statements. Some reviews read like they were written by publishers of competing apps.

This clutter and disinformation can make it hard to find quality apps. If you're new to the App Store, stick to the Top Charts screen for your first shopping spree. After a few cases of buyer's regret (it happens to everybody), you'll learn to separate the wheat from the chaff.

Some excellent apps are mentioned elsewhere in this book, such as the iOS version of iLife (iPhoto, iMovie, and GarageBand). Also, some big shots have their own apps, including Amazon, Facebook, Twitter, Skype, Dropbox, Netflix, and Yelp. This chapter shows a tiny slice of what's available.

In This Chapter

iWork

The iOS version of Apple's iWork suite lacks the horsepower and features of iWork for Mac and Microsoft Office, and it isn't meant to replace them. But it's tuned to work with iOS's multitouch interface and delivers what you expect from office software: templates, editing and formatting tools, tables, charts, file sharing, and file conversion (including compatibility with Excel, Word, and PowerPoint). iWork also lets you embellish your documents with photos, movies, text boxes, and shapes. The apps Ⓐ—Numbers for spreadsheets, Pages for word processing, and Keynote for presentations—are sold separately.

TIP If you need to create text-only documents, try iA Writer, a text editor that's superior to Notes (see Chapter 17) but without the bells and whistles of Pages.

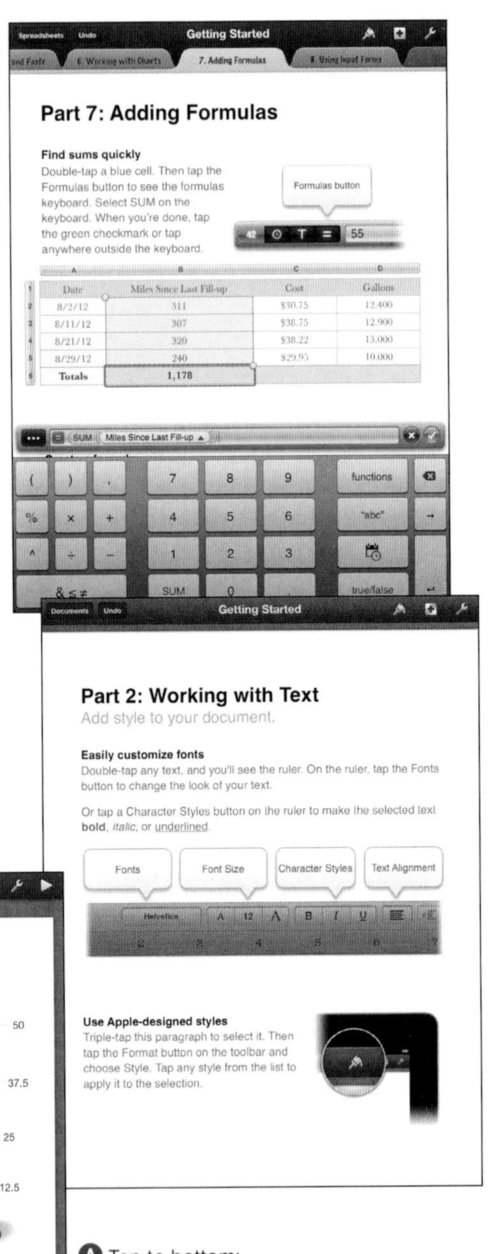

Miles Since Last Fill-up

8/2/12 311 $30.75 12.400
8/11/12 307 $38.75 12.900
8/21/12 320 $38.22 13.000
8/29/12 240 $29.95 10.000
Totals 1,178

Miles Since Last Fill-up

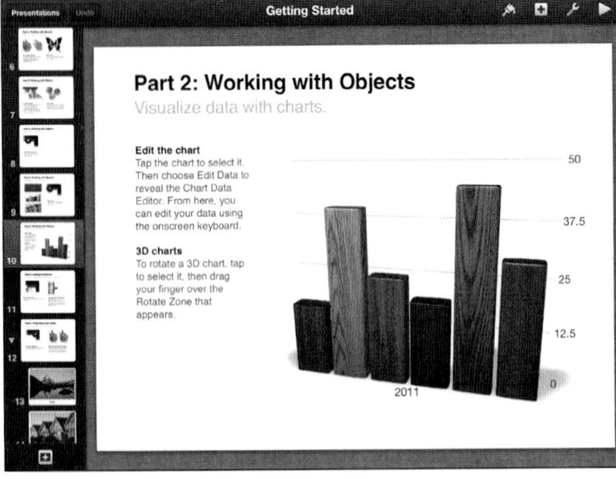

Character Styles

Use Apple-designed styles
Triple-tap this paragraph to select it. Then tap the Format button on the toolbar and choose Style. Tap any style from the list to apply it to the selection.

Presentations
Getting Started
7. Adding Formulas
Part 7: Adding Formulas
Find sums quickly
Double-tap a blue cell. Then tap the Formulas button to see the formulas keyboard. Select SUM on the keyboard. When you're done, tap the green checkmark or tap anywhere outside the keyboard.
Formulas button
Easily customize fonts
Double-tap any text, and you'll see the ruler. On the ruler, tap the Fonts button to change the look of your text.
Or tap a Character Styles button on the ruler to make the selected text bold, italic, or underlined.
Part 2: Working with Objects
Visualize data with charts.
Edit the chart
Tap the chart to select it. Then choose Edit Data to reveal the Chart Data Editor. From here, you can edit your data using the onscreen keyboard.
3D charts
To rotate a 3D chart, tap to select it, then drag your finger over the Rotate Zone that appears.
50
37.5
25
12.5
0
2011

Ⓐ Top to bottom: Numbers, Pages, and Keynote.

GoodReader

iBooks (see Chapter 11) is a great app for reading EPUB-format books, but when it comes to using it for reading PDF files, the word *adequate* comes to mind. If you have a large collection of PDFs, consider GoodReader **A**, a robust reading app that lets you open huge PDF files; highlight and annotate PDFs; read Office, iWork, and HTML files; sync with remote servers (including Dropbox, SugarSync, and FTP); organize your library in folders; and more.

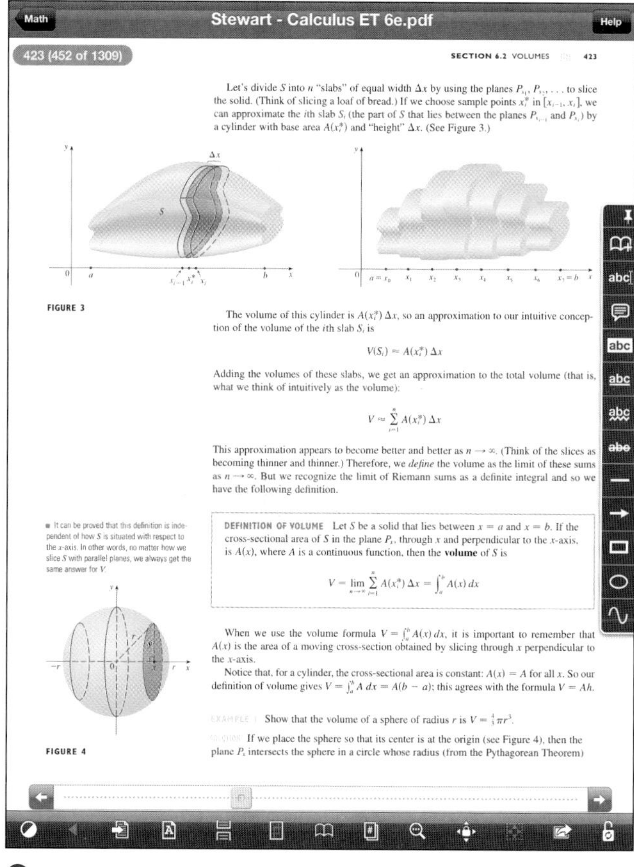

A GoodReader.

Google Earth

Google Earth (A) features satellite images and aerial photos merged into a virtual globe. You can "fly" to any place around the world and toggle various layers to superimpose place names, businesses, shared photos, Wikipedia articles, and more. You can pan, zoom, rotate, and tilt the maps.

The Google Earth gallery offers additional layers—such as country tours, earthquake maps, surfing spots, and hurricane paths—shared by people around the world.

TIP Several other free Google apps are available, including Gmail, Google Play Books, and Google Search. The latter is a stand-alone app—separate from the Google search feature in Safari—and is a bit like having the Google Chrome browser on your iPad.

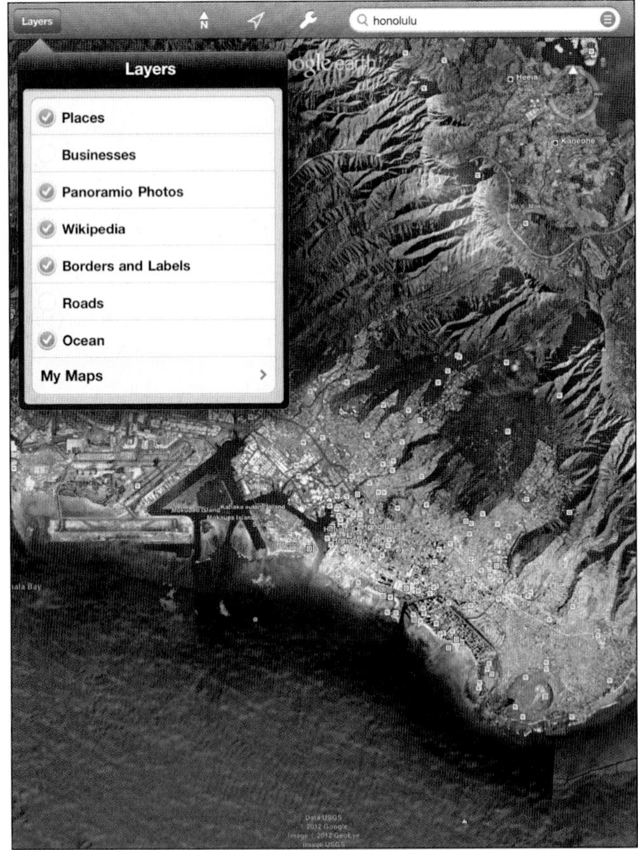

(A) Google Earth.

Trulia

Trulia **A** is a real-estate search engine that makes finding a new place to buy or rent less intimidating. You can poke around to find apartments and houses, complete with photos, prices, tax info, and other property facts.

TIP A similar app is available from Zillow, another respected name in real-estate search.

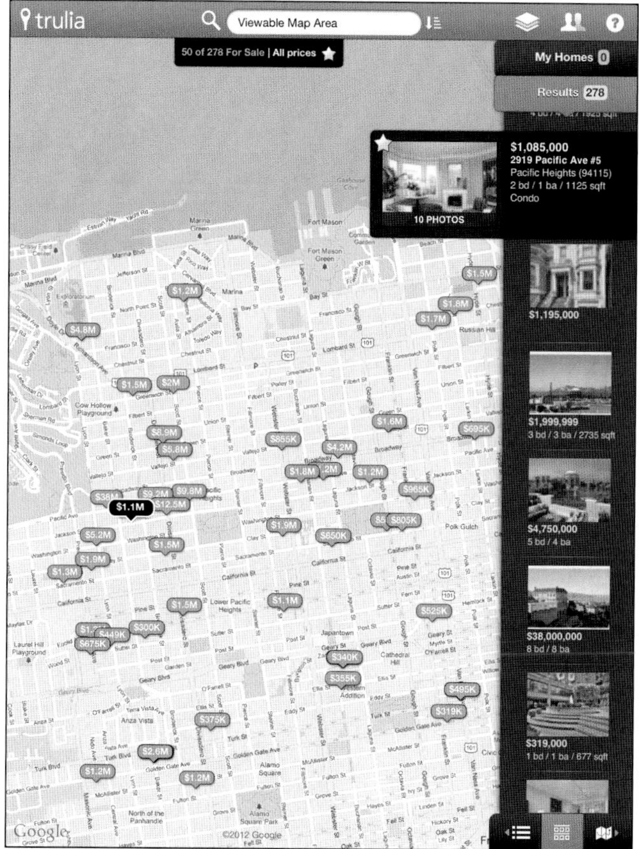

A Trulia.

Angry Birds

This strategy puzzle game has clung like a barnacle to the top of the charts since its introduction. Game play is simple: Catapult kamikaze birds into the rickety strongholds of thieving pigs Ⓐ. The addictive challenge comes from the game's physics. You must figure out the right speed and trajectory at which to slingshot the birds so that they collapse increasingly complex structures onto the pigs.

TIP Several special editions of Angry Birds are also available, including Angry Birds Seasons, Angry Birds Rio, and Angry Birds Space.

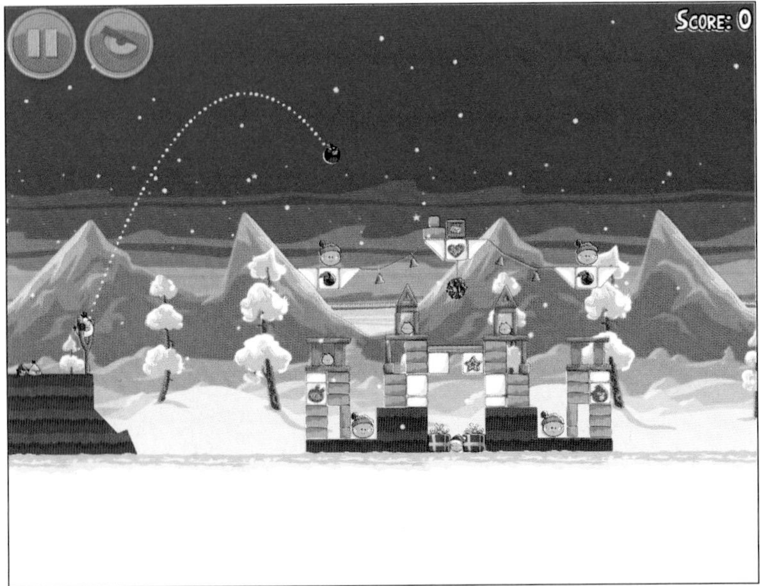

Ⓐ Angry Birds.

Paper

Paper **A** lets you sketch diagrams, illustrations, drawings, and notes, and then share them across the Web. A simple interface masks a sophisticated drawing engine that makes it surprisingly easy to write, sketch, and color. You can arrange your works in virtual notebooks or journals, just like real artists and hipsters do.

TIP Another popular sketching and handwriting app is Penultimate.

A Paper.

Azul Media Player

If you download a video, movie, or TV show from the Internet, chances are that it won't be in one of iOS's native formats. Converting a video to an iPad-friendly format is a time-consuming hassle. Instead, use a third-party player like Azul Media Player **A**, which can play just about any viable format you throw at it, including AVI, FLV, MKV, MP4, and WMV.

Media players make great travel apps because you can copy movies to your iPad and play them without an Internet connection (see "Copying Files Between Your iPad and Your Computer" in Chapter 4). Azul also supports AirPlay and can stream videos from the Web.

TIP The App Store is awash with media players. One popular alternative to Azul is GoodPlayer.

A Azul Media Player.

Index

K

L

M

N

S

T

U

V

W

Y